Beyond the Crescent Curtain

Beyond the Crescent Curtain

GOD REVEALING HIMSELF TO
THE PEOPLE OF THE MIDDLE EAST

David LeCompte

BEYOND THE CRESCENT CURTAIN
PUBLISHED BY In His Fields Publications
www.inhisfieldspublications.com

All Scripture quotations, unless otherwise indicated, are taken from
the Holy Bible, New International Version®. NIV®. Copyright
© 1973, 1978, 1984 by International Bible Society. Used by
permission of Zondervan Publishing House. All rights reserved.

Italics in Scripture quotations reflect the author's added emphasis.

Names and identifying details in anecdotes and stories have been
changed to protect the identities of the persons involved.

ISBN-13 978-0-9842177-4-8 (trade paper)
ISBN-10 0-9842177-4-8 (trade paper)

Copyright © 2010 by David LeCompte
All interior and cover photos © 2010 by David LeCompte
Book cover design © 2010 by Connie Beecher
Map design © 2010 by Connie Beecher
Interior design © 2010 by Nathan Fisher, www.nathanfisher.net
Back cover author photo © 2010 by Show the Story Photography
Publishing and marketing support provided by:
Jeff Pederson at JPED Publishing Group, www.jpedpublishing.com

Library of Congress Cataloging-in-Publication Data
LeCompte, David
Beyond the Crescent Curtain: God Revealing Himself To The
People of the Middle East

Printed in the United States of America
2010—First Edition

Contents

"As someone who has traveled with David LeCompte in the Middle East, I have seen firsthand his love for the Muslim world. This passion, combined with experience and insight, fuels a unique perspective on the world of Islam and the growing Christian church among Muslim communities. Through the use of snapshot glimpses into history, current affairs, biblical narrative and personal encounters, Beyond the Crescent Curtain confronts fear and misunderstanding, and will leave you with a profound respect for Christians living in Muslim countries and will encourage you with a practical message of hope and the need for a loving response to the Islamic world."

—ART DYKSTRA, MISSIONS AND OUTREACH PASTOR, CALVARY CHAPEL ST. PETERSBURG, PINELLAS PARK, FL

Dedication

To my brothers and sisters in Christ from the Middle East—thank you for sharing your lives and stories with me. Without you, this book would not have been written.

To my loving wife and family for joining me on this journey.
I couldn't have made it without you.

Issa—You are the reason for it all!

Acknowledgments

To my editor, Jennifer Lonas—thank you for your endless patience and tireless input to help craft and mold my thoughts—and my sometimes wandering words. I couldn't have finished this project without you.

To Dr. Don McCurry—your years of wisdom and encouragement mean so much to me. In the short time we have known each other, your passion to see Muslims come to Christ has inspired me like no one else I have ever met.

To Jeff Pedersen and his team at JPED Publishing—thank you for helping me share this message with the world.

To those who have shared their lives with me in this journey—sleeping in strange hotels, eating ethnic meals, and riding in planes, taxis, and other modes of transportation to live out our faith among the nations—thanks for being comrades!

To Vincent—for your friendship and encouragement over the years.

And to my best friend, Jesus—thank You for leading me on this pathway.

Foreword

David LeCompte has gone where few others have dared to go. Starting in Grozny, Chechnya (southern Russia), building an orphanage, this intrepid apostle of love has moved and ministered in some most unlikely places: Mashhad, Tehran, Mosul, Yalova, Muslim Jerusalem, Ramallah, Bethlehem, Khartoum, Cairo and border towns in Kurdistan - Iraq.

In each place, David has found God at work in the midst of wars, earthquakes, ethnic cleansings and among refugees. Through the eyes of this gifted storyteller, you will meet believers among the Kurds, the Shias, the Sunnis, the Sufis in such lands as Iraq, Iran, Jordan, Turkey, Lebanon, Egypt, Sudan, Israel and the West Bank.

Through this marvelous account of God at work in the most unexpected places, you will find a rich mine of insight on Muslim culture and customs interwoven with well-researched historical background material on the places visited that sweep the historical and political landscape of the Middle East.

Choosing saints from one end of the Scriptures to the other, the author has deftly woven these cameo studies into a beautiful tapestry of God's love, past and present, including angel visitants and dreams as relevant today as in ages past.

I highly recommend this book which leads you to look behind the veil of western prejudices to see the human faces of

Iranians, Iraqis, Kurds, Palestinians, Sudanese, Turks, Egyptians and Palestinians who have forsaken Islam to come to Jesus. And be ready to shed a few tears and give some shouts of joy as you read the story of God's glory at work in the midst of the most improbable places.

Dr. Don McCurry, President
Ministries To Muslims

Preface

On a bitterly cold day in January 1997, I boarded a train heading to the North Caucasus region of southern Russia. The two-day journey through the Russian countryside would transport me to an area close to the border of Chechnya—one of my first real encounters with Muslim war refugees from that conflict-ravaged republic.

Arriving in Nalchik, a city in the Russian republic of Karbardino-Balkariya, I visited many Chechen refugees who had fled the conflict in their homeland, less than fifty miles away. Huddling together in rat-infested, Soviet-era sanatoriums, they struggled to survive the harsh Russian winter.

As I listened to their stories of horror and injustice, I felt God tug on my heart, and I knew I had to see firsthand the humanitarian tragedy taking place in Ichkeria, the land of the Chechens.

A few days later, I attempted to cross into the Chechen Republic at the Ingushetia-Chechnya border crossing, an hour's drive south of Nalchik. But Russian border guards refused to let me pass through the checkpoint. Disappointed but not deterred, I returned to the United States, determined to find another way to accomplish my goal of sharing God's love with Muslims in Chechnya.

Four months after my first attempt to visit the Chechen Republic, I traveled back to that same border crossing with a small group of volunteers, a videographer, two large trucks of humanitarian aid, and an official document verifying that I was a guest of the Ministry of Islamic Religious Affairs in Chechnya.

Waiting at the checkpoint with my team, I watched a military Jeep and four other vehicles speed up the road in typical Caucasus fashion. The vehicles slid to a halt in a swirling cloud of dust, and robust men in Gucci suits, wearing Ray-Ban sunglasses and military fatigues, leaped out with Kalashnikov automatic machine guns at the ready. They looked more like Chechen rebels and Russian mafia than religious Sufi Muslims.

"As-salaam aleikum," one of the men said, introducing himself and his colleagues as representatives from the Religious Affairs office.

Within minutes, our group piled into one of the Jeeps and held on for a bare-knuckled ride to the Chechen capitol of Grozny. Speeding along with reckless abandon, our driver wove his way through a slalom course of massive asphalt craters and potholes created by the rockets and Grad missiles that Russia had rained down on the tiny republic. Some craters were large enough to swallow a small car; sadly some already had. Treetops shredded by rockets from Russian helicopter gunships lined the road all the way to the outskirts of Grozny. Devastation stretched as far as the eye could see.

As we approached the capitol city, one of the armed men in our Jeep leaned out the window, pointed his automatic rifle into the air, and started shooting—the Chechen way of stopping traffic so our little convoy could pass through the intersections. There weren't any traffic signals; in fact, there weren't any streetlights, electric poles, or electricity. Everything had been bombed flat.

Entering Grozny from the south, we passed through what was left of the once-famous Minutka Square. Row upon row of multistory apartment buildings resembled stacks of concrete pancakes.

Thousands of Russian and Chechen civilians were entombed beneath the mountains of rubble and shredded metal. Most would never be found, their bones returning to the ground from which they came—ashes to ashes, dust to dust.

Burned-out skeletons of Russian tanks littered the roadsides, monuments to the Russian and Chechen fighters who had shed their blood just a few months earlier. Our driver commented proudly that the streets were much cleaner than they had been just a few weeks prior to our visit.

Staring out the window at the devastation of war, I was moved beyond words. I couldn't imagine what it would be like to live in this bombed-out shell of a city. Since 1994, the bloody conflict between Russia's massive military and the Chechen *shahid* (Islamic warriors) had been raging unabated, and the civilian death toll among Chechens and Russians had climbed to more than ninety thousand by the end of 1996. Systematic ethnic cleansings throughout Chechnya bordered on genocide, and more than five hundred thousand Chechen refugees had fled to the neighboring republics of Ingushetia, Dagestan, Karbardino-Balkariya, and other parts of the North Caucasus.

People back in the United States wondered why I would choose to work in one of the most dangerous places on earth. I was well aware of the risks, but I also believed that in this place of violence, suffering, and death, God would open doors for me to shine His light into the darkness and reflect the love of Christ to Muslims and Russians alike. I knew that where the darkness is greatest, God's light often shines the brightest.

The war in Chechnya had created an opportunity for me to

genuinely live out my faith as a follower of Christ among the Sufi Muslim population. When bombs were falling and children were dying in the streets, it didn't matter to the Chechens if I had my biblical theology straight or could recite Scripture. What mattered most to them was that I cared.

As I traveled across this deeply scarred land, praying my way through Russian military checkpoints and Chechen militia roadblocks, venturing where few would dare to go, I knew I was exactly where God wanted me to be. In this little corner of hell, God gripped my heart with a passion to reach out to Muslims and build bridges of friendship and trust so that one day I might share the hope and love of Christ with them.

During those first days in Chechnya, with Russian rockets screaming overhead and Kalashnikov automatic rifles echoing in the night, I shared bread and roasted lamb with Muslim families as we sat talking around diesel-powered generators in dimly lit rooms. My heart broke as my Ukrainian translator related their stories of hardship and suffering, and in turn shared with them my vision of building an orphanage near Grozny that would bring hope to Chechen children.

Deeply moved by my compassion for their children, several local Chechen families committed to help oversee the construction of the orphanage and staff the facility when it opened its doors to the community. During the nine years I served as director, their courageous and tireless efforts enabled us to provide shelter for more than sixty children and offer maternity care and food to thousands of pregnant mothers and their babies. In His Fields, the nonprofit organization I established, supplied financial and material support through individual sponsors and volunteers from America. Risking their lives, these volunteers joined me on regular visits to the orphanage, where we witnessed the transforming power of God's love as we lived out our faith among the Muslim people of Chechnya. We even experienced the joy of seeing two staff members at the orphanage and one of the children accept Issa (Jesus) and start a lifelong journey of following Him.

In that dark corner of the world, I realized that many Muslims are born into the Islamic faith through a centuries-old ethnic heritage. Being Muslim is an inherent part of their identity, not a matter of free choice. They grow up learning that their religion demands submission to an impersonal God as well as strict compliance to the five pillars of Islam: bearing witness that Allah is the only God, praying at least five times a day, giving alms, fasting during the month of Ramadan, and making a pilgrimage to Mecca. Most Muslims have practiced these requirements from childhood—and even know about Jesus (Issa) from the Koran—and yet they are no closer to knowing the God they so diligently worship or having a personal relationship with Him. This is especially true of the Chechen people, who practice a mystical form of folk Islam as Sufi Muslims.

Since those life-changing years of ministry, I have dedicated my life to sharing the love of Christ with Muslims around the world. I have visited war zones and refugee camps in Albania and Kosovo, underground house churches of persecuted Christians in Iran and China, and earthquake-devastated Kurdish refugee communities in Turkey. I've traveled across hazardous mountain passes in Armenia, visited Palestinian believers in the squalid refugee camps of the West Bank, toured poverty-stricken villages in Egypt and Sudan, and most recently, visited the ancient land of Iraq, where God first appeared to Abram.

Even when Islamic terrorists attacked the World Trade Center on September 11, 2001, killing thousands of innocent Americans and igniting the global war on terror, I continued my work among the Muslim people. My heart for the Muslim world hasn't changed, because God's heart for people never changes, regardless of their ethnic or religious backgrounds. In fact, my desire to see the *other* sons of Abraham—Ishmael's descendants—come to faith in Christ is stronger and more passionate today than ever!

Raised in Alabama during the racially explosive civil rights era in America, I witnessed firsthand the deeply entrenched racial prejudice against people of color in the South. Like many of my young peers, I rejected the attitudes that for generations have made racism acceptable in our culture—even in the church—and I stood up for those suffering discrimination and abuse because of their ethnic heritage. Through that experience, God prepared my heart to work among the Muslim people, whom many in the Western world have come to fear and unjustly despise.

I often feel as if I'm walking in the footsteps of Jesus, who reached out to the despised people of his day, like the Samaritans. To the Jews, the Samaritan people were a race of half-breeds, stepchildren. They weren't considered true descendants of Abraham, and associating with them was an unthinkable defilement. In fact, Jews and Samaritans harbored an ancient hatred for one another extending back to Old Testament times. But Jesus saw the Samaritan people in a radically different way. He willingly reached out to them, reflecting God's heart for all people and showing that everyone who comes to Him in faith is welcome in the kingdom of God!

Like the Samaritans, the Muslim people of the twenty-first century are often looked upon with disdain. But I have no doubt that if Jesus were walking the dusty streets of the Middle East today, He would treat Muslims with the same love and compassion He showed the Samaritan people.

The Muslim world is my Samaria, and as I've traveled throughout the Middle East for more than a decade, I've seen the hand of God transforming hearts and lives. Abraham's descendants are coming to faith in Christ! But sadly, the Western church is largely unaware of this incredible move of God. The fields in the Middle East are "ripe for harvest" (John 4:35), but many Christians in America don't have a clue about what God is doing there. In fact, since 9/11, it seems that many believers have come to view the Muslim world with hostility and suspicion.

Whether we have been influenced by the overwhelmingly negative media coverage of the Islamic world, hardened by the grief of losing a friend or loved one in the war on terror, or perhaps swept up in a whirlwind of patriotic fervor, I believe that any hatred or prejudice we harbor against Muslims grieves the heart of God. Jesus died for all people, regardless of ethnicity or religion, and He longs for all to be saved—even those who carry out murderous acts of terrorism.

My vision for writing a book about God's transforming work in the Middle East began to grow shortly after 9/11. In my travels around the country, I've heard the rage many Americans feel toward Islamic extremists and have seen roots of prejudice growing against all Muslims. This attitude has even worked its way into the Christian church.

I truly understand the outrage over what happened on 9/11—I've struggled with it myself—but as followers of Christ, we can't give in to the temptation to hate Muslims or lump them all into one category. We need to see the Muslim people from God's perspective and learn what it means to love our enemies as Jesus commanded. Not all Muslims are radical, gun-wielding jihadists looking to kill American infidels. Most of them just want to live in peace—like you and me. They are human beings created in the image of God and need to experience His love and grace.

Since 9/11, I've felt compelled to challenge the beliefs and perceptions that many American Christians have about Muslims and to share from personal experience a biblical perspective that I believe is lacking in the church today. This book is the culmination of that effort. It is the fruit of frequent visits to the Middle East, amazing stories of God revealing Himself to those who are crying out to know Him, and abundant opportunities to share His heart for the Middle East with churches across America.

In the following chapters, you'll walk with me through dusty streets in exotic lands; into mosques and marketplaces, homes and churches; along mountain passes and into war zones. You'll meet real people who have jobs and families, hopes and dreams, and most of all, a longing to know God. Their stories will touch you as you identify with their joys, their sorrows, their fears, their suffering. You'll also meet people who came to faith in Jesus in some amazing ways, whether through dreams and visions, unlikely encounters, life-threatening circumstances, or the miraculous gift of an Arabic Bible.* Each real-life story offers a powerful illustration of God's ability to reach those we might think are unreachable and to change even the hardest hearts. Nothing is impossible for Him (Luke 18:27)!

Following each story is a commentary section that may include biblical, historical, sociopolitical, or cultural background to enrich your understanding, to provide additional context, and to stimulate discussion about controversial issues like racism. I realize that my commentary may elicit a wide range of reactions and may even offend some readers. However, my intention is not to offend but to present a perspective readers may not have considered before. I believe so strongly that Christians in the Western church need to bring issues like racism and our attitudes toward Muslims into the light of God's truth that I'm willing to risk offending some people.

Although my views have been forged over many years as I've interacted with Muslims around the world, I don't consider myself an expert on the Islamic faith and its various expressions. Likewise, I discuss biblical concepts and events primarily from a layman's point of view. Although I have taken care to ensure accuracy and integrity when referring to Scripture, I have at times taken interpretive liberties and have embellished some biblical accounts to describe events that could have taken place or to reflect what people may have thought or felt. Whenever you encounter a familiar Bible story in the pages that follow, I want you to think not in lofty theological terms but of real people in real-life situations. The marketplace of life is where God makes Himself real to us!

It is my prayer that as you read this book, the Lord will awaken you to the incredible things He is doing in the Middle East today and that He will soften your heart toward the Muslim people, filling you with His love and enabling you to see them through His eyes. Above all, I pray that as you ponder the message of this book, God will ignite a fire within you like the one He ignited in me so many years ago when He called me to share His love with Muslims around the world.

Jesus said to His disciples, "Open your eyes and look at the fields! They are ripe for harvest" (John 4:35). The fields in the Middle East are ripe, but the workers are very, very few. It's time to open our eyes and be involved in this great harvest!

---

*   *Although most of these courageous believers would prefer that I use their real names and locations, I have altered details in most stories to protect their identities and ministries.*

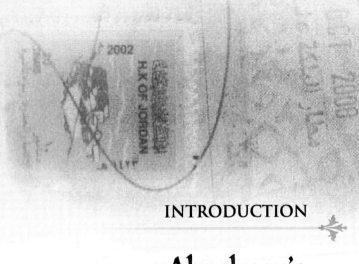

INTRODUCTION

Abraham's Forgotten Son

On a warm summer evening, under a soft moonlit sky in the desert valley near Hebron, two veiled women moved silently through the camp, past smoldering fires and darkened tents.[1] At the entrance to one of the tents, Sarai hesitated, glancing at her Egyptian maidservant Hagar. Years had passed since the day God appeared to Sarai's husband, Abram, promising to bless him with a son who would one day inherit his estate, including all of his wealth, property, and possessions. Yet Sarai remained childless—and neither she nor Abram was getting any younger. After all these years, God showed no signs of fulfilling His promise. What else could Sarai do but offer her maidservant to Abram to bear the son she could never give him?[2]

She sighed deeply as she entered Abram's tent. Hagar stood uncertainly beside her mistress, lowering her eyes to the ground as

Sarai presented her to Abram. The flickering candlelight accentuated the beauty of Hagar's olive eyes and dark copper skin. She was young and vibrant, especially for the eighty-five-year-old Abram. Sarai gazed into her husband's eyes and nodded encouragingly before slipping through the tent flap and disappearing into the darkness.

In a night of tenderness and passion, Abram lay with Hagar. From the time he had brought Hagar out of Egypt to serve his household, Abram had been her covering and protection, the very source of Hagar's life. Now, in an ironic twist of fate, she had given him new life, restoring his dwindling hope, offering a way to fulfill God's promise—the promise of a son. Through Hagar, Abram's deepest longings might at last be satisfied. She was no longer merely Sarai's maidservant, a gift from the pharaoh of Egypt,[3] or the woman who fed the livestock and cooked for Abram's hired hands.

In the months that followed, Hagar confirmed what everyone else in the camp already suspected: She was pregnant. Abram's heart leaped when he heard the news. He would finally be a father! The impossible had happened.

The men in camp were quick to congratulate Abram, slapping him on the back and teasing him about his age. The women praised God with shouts of joy. But not everyone was thrilled with the news. Sarai watched the festivities from a distance, a frown creasing her brow. Instead of the joy she had anticipated, she felt great jealousy and shame at the sight of Hagar.

Sarai thought back wistfully to the early days when she and Abram left Egypt with the young maidservant. Sarai had felt compassion for Hagar, who had been torn away from everything she had ever known to serve foreigners in a foreign land. After serving in

Pharaoh's court in relative comfort all her life, Hagar had found such a vast wilderness of blistering heat, wild animals, and rugged terrain an unbearable trial. Sarai had been gentle with Hagar in those days, helping her adjust to the harsh nomadic lifestyle in a barren desert. And yet Sarai often found the young girl weeping.

But in time, Hagar's spirits seemed to recover, and the women began to enjoy a warm camaraderie. It seemed they had been destined to share their lives on this strange journey that had taken them far from their families and the comforts of home. Sarai fondly remembered how she and Hagar had loved to shop for silk pillows and elaborately woven carpets in the local markets, a diversion Abram had little interest in. The women had passed many happy hours sipping cups of sweet tea and munching on cashews, palm dates, and figs. These simple pleasures had been a favorite way of breaking up the long, monotonous days in the Arabian Desert and easing Hagar's grief.

Sarai understood homesickness all too well. She missed the comfortable life she had left behind in Ur, a bustling city on the banks of the Euphrates River in Babylon, but the companionship of her maidservant had soothed her own homesickness.

Yet now that Hagar was carrying Abram's child, she despised her mistress, making Sarai's life a misery. As the weeks passed, Hagar began to neglect her duties and glared at Sarai in stony silence whenever her mistress was nearby. One day Sarai lashed out at her husband, blaming him for her problems with her maidservant.

"I gave you my servant," she complained, "and now that she's pregnant, she hates me and won't give me a moment's peace. The Lord knows this is your fault!"

Day after day, Sarai pressured Abram to do something about the situation. When her nagging became intolerable, he reluctantly gave her permission to do as she pleased with Hagar.

"She is your handmaid," he sighed. "Do whatever you feel is best."

From that moment on, Sarai began to treat her maidservant harshly.

Desperate to escape the scorn of her mistress, Hagar fled into the Sinai Desert before daybreak one morning. Exposed to the elements and vulnerable to bandits, she knew the desert was no place for a woman in her condition. And yet how could she return to her mistress? Thoughts of the abuse she had endured brought tears to her eyes.

By day's end, the scorching sun and harsh wind had taken their toll. Exhausted from heat and thirst, Hagar collapsed by the roadside near a small spring of water seeping from the ground. Alone and afraid, she cried out, "Oh God of my master, Abram! Do You see me here in this desert place? Is this the way You have ordained my life to end? I have faithfully served my master all these years, and I have seen how You answered him in his moments of despair. You watched over him in Egypt when Pharaoh could have taken his life. And yet You spared him! Why did You choose me, a mere servant girl in Pharaoh's house, to bear this man's child?

The desert sun pierced the sky like a giant laser, beating down relentlessly on Hagar. She lowered her cracked lips to the sand and sipped at the meager trickle of water flowing from the spring. Lifting her head, she squinted into the sun as hazy images appeared on the horizon. Abram and Sarai came into view, leading their enormous caravan of horses, camels, and carts out of the Valley of the Pharaohs in Egypt. Everyone was laughing; Abram and Sarai seemed so happy. They were returning to the land God had called them to. Hagar was riding on a milk-white camel next to Sarai. She joined in the laughter as she ventured into a new life with her foreign masters.

Hagar smiled as she recalled those days. Then like a ghost, the image vanished. Was she losing her mind? She collapsed on the ground, her body convulsing with sobs. She licked her bleeding lips as the blowing sand stung her eyes.

Again she cried out, "Oh God of my master, Abram! Why have I been punished for obeying my mistress and satisfying my master's desires? Is he not pleased that I have conceived a son who will be my master's heir? Will You now kill me and my child in this desert? Surely You are a God of compassion!"

As Hagar lifted her eyes once more, she envisioned the night she had entered Abram's tent. She remembered how shy and nervous she had felt when she offered herself to her master. The exploits of this warrior from Ur were known far and wide. With more than three hundred men of valor, he had defeated the five kings of Sodom and rescued his cousin Lot from their wicked hands. Abram was also a very rich man, amassing great wealth as the Lord his God blessed him. Such a man could have had his pick of women. Why had he agreed to take Hagar into his harem?

That night, the smell of incense had permeated Abram's tent as Hagar and Abram embraced in the flickering candlelight. He had been gentle, and she could still hear the words he had whispered softly in her ear: "Sarai has not conceived these many years. God promised that He would bless me with an heir. Perhaps tonight my God will bless us, and we will see this come to pass."

It seemed impossible, and yet in a moment of warmth and tenderness, Hagar's lord and master became her lover—and the father of her child. It was a night she would remember for the rest of her life.

The vision faded, and Hagar realized it had been another mirage. Tears streamed down her cheeks, evaporating as they dropped onto the burning sand. How long before she would die in this godforsaken place?

Suddenly a voice broke into her anguish. "Where are you coming from and where are you going, Hagar?"

Hagar looked up and saw a man in dazzling white robes standing in front of her. She rubbed her eyes, thinking she was seeing another vision. But this was no mirage.

"I have run away from my mistress," Hagar answered, trembling with fear.

"You must return to Sarai and submit yourself to her," the angel commanded.

Tears flooded Hagar's eyes as the hope in her heart began to wither. But the angel continued, "I will make your descendants too numerous to count. The son you are carrying will be called Ishmael, for God has heard of your affliction. Ishmael will be a wild donkey of a man, and he will live in conflict and hostility with everyone."

In astonishment, Hagar whispered, "El Roi! My eyes have seen the One who sees me!"

Greatly encouraged by God's promise, Hagar returned to her mistress and recounted to Abram and Sarai all the angel of the Lord had spoken to her in the desert. Abram believed the message, and when Hagar gave birth, he named his firstborn son Ishmael, just as the angel had instructed. At long last, God had fulfilled His promise to Abram, blessing him with an heir at the age of eighty-six.

Ishmael was the pride and joy of his father. Abram doted on the boy, and the two quickly became inseparable companions. They often sat outside Abram's tent as Abram recounted his days in Ur, when Jehovah first appeared to him and called him to leave his homeland. Whenever Abram told his son stories about his life and faith, Ishmael hung on every word.

As the child grew, Abram taught Ishmael how to tend the livestock and perform other chores, praising him lavishly for his efforts to please his father. Abram also prepared young Ishmael to become a mighty warrior like his father, teaching him to ride a horse, shoot with a bow, wield a sword, and carry a shield. Abram even let his son gather the firewood and prepare the animals for the altar where Abram offered sacrifices to his God Jehovah.

When Ishmael was old enough, Abram began to groom him to assume all the responsibilities and privileges of the family heir. Ishmael glowed with pride over the trust his father placed in him.

Then one day, God appeared to Abram and made a covenant with him, saying, "From this time forward, you will be called Abraham, for you will be the father of many nations. Your descendants will be too numerous to count, and this land will be their possession forever."

Recalling God's promise many years before, Abraham thought of his son, Ishmael. The Lord had fulfilled His promise to give Abraham an heir, and now his son was destined for great things. But then God declared, "You are to call your wife Sarah from now on. I will bless her as a mother of nations and will give her a son. He will become a great nation, and I will establish an everlasting covenant with him and his descendants."

Stunned, Abraham fell to the ground in worship. *How can this be?* he thought, chuckling to himself. *I am ninety-nine years old, and Sarah will soon be ninety. We are dried out old stumps, and Sarah is well beyond the age of bearing children.*

Then he said aloud, "Oh, Lord, I will be content if only You will bless my son, Ishmael, and grant him favor in Your sight."

But God replied, "Your wife, Sarah, will bear a son this time next year, and you will call his name Isaac. I will establish My covenant with him, and from him will arise twelve rulers. Nevertheless, I will also bless your son, Ishmael, and will make him into a great nation."

That day, Abraham honored God's command and circumcised every male in his household as a sign of the covenant the Lord had established with him. Abraham and Ishmael, who was thirteen years of age by this time, were also circumcised.

Shortly after this, three strangers appeared in the camp and approached Abraham as he sat at the entrance to his tent. Abraham quickly rose and greeted his guests according to Middle Eastern custom, inviting the men to sit while servants brought a basin of water to wash their feet. Some other servants killed a choice calf from the herd and roasted it over a fire while Sarah baked loaves of flatbread.

When the meal had been set before his guests, Abraham asked, "Where are you from, my friends? Have you come here on business?"

The men replied, "We have come to tell you that this time next year, your wife, Sarah, will give birth to a son."

Eavesdropping inside the tent, Sarah laughed under her breath in disbelief. *I am a barren old woman,* she said to herself, *and my husband's seed has dried up as well. These men must be out of their minds to make such a ridiculous claim!*

The Lord heard Sarah's laughter and said to Abraham, "Is anything too difficult for Me to perform? Just as I promised, Sarah will have a son, and I will return next year at this time when he is born."

Soon after this, Sarah became pregnant. When she told Abraham the news, he took her in his arms, and they both wept for joy. God had finally taken away the disgrace of her barrenness.

As word spread throughout the camp, Hagar pondered what this might mean. Ishmael was Abraham's firstborn son and the rightful heir of his father's estate. But he was also the son of a servant woman, not the natural-born son of Abraham's wife, Sarah. Hagar had heard whisperings around the camp about the promise God had made to Abraham, and fear gripped her heart as she realized that this child of promise might one day steal the inheritance away from her own son.

Now that Sarah was carrying a child of her own, she treated Hagar with even greater contempt. The glint in Sarah's eye and the set of her lips spoke volumes whenever she looked in Hagar's direction. The two women avoided each other as much as possible as the months passed. Abraham seemed increasingly distracted with the impending birth, and Hagar had a foreboding sense that everything would change when the child arrived.

Late one night, Hagar heard a commotion in the camp. Rising from her bed, she rushed to the tent flap and peered outside. A crowd had gathered outside Sarah's tent, and more people were arriving by the minute. Hagar wandered over toward the tent and listened as the women whispered to one another in excited voices. As she had suspected, her mistress was in labor. A great darkness enveloped Hagar. Shivering, she looked up at the sky and breathed a silent prayer to the God who spoke to her in the desert: *Please don't remove Your blessing from my son!*

Sarah laughed as she nursed her newborn son. What the visitors had told Abraham the year before had indeed come true. Abraham peeked through the opening of the tent, and she waved him inside. Beaming from ear to ear, he gazed at his son, filled with awe that God had fulfilled His promise after so many years. Abraham extended a callused hand and grasped one of Isaac's tiny fingers. Tears trickled down Abraham's face as he turned to look into his wife's eyes. They gazed at each other for a long moment and then burst into laughter.

When the day arrived for Isaac to be weaned, Abraham threw a huge party, inviting everyone from the surrounding countryside to the celebration. During the festivities, Sarah noticed Hagar scoffing at her. Furious, she took her husband aside and demanded that he cast Hagar and Ishmael out of the family once and for all.

"That slave woman and her son have no right to the inheritance that belongs to Isaac," Sarah insisted.

Her cutting words broke Abraham's heart. After the party, he withdrew to his tent to pray about the situation. How could he send away his firstborn son, the joy of his life for thirteen years? He loved Ishmael, and the bond they had formed as father and son could never be broken. *I've poured my very life into the boy all these years,* Abraham reasoned, *and he is fully prepared to accept the rights and responsibilities of my estate. I can't go back on my word now!*

Late into the night, Abraham paced back and forth in his tent, crying out to God for wisdom. The answer God gave the patriarch was not entirely unexpected, and yet it deeply distressed him.

"Listen to Sarah," the Lord told him. "I will watch over Ishmael and his mother, and he will become the father of a great nation."

Long before sunrise, Abraham stepped from his tent after a sleepless night of wrestling with God over the plight of Hagar and his teenage son. Even though God had promised to take care of them, Abraham couldn't bear the thought of sending them away.

Tears rolled down his cheeks as he wrapped a few pieces of flatbread into a headscarf and then walked slowly over to a well to fill a goatskin with fresh water. A servant brought Hagar and Ishmael to Abraham, and his voice broke as he told them of his decision. In the early morning light, Abraham gently placed his arm around Hagar and escorted her and Ishmael to the edge of the oasis. After giving his son a fatherly embrace and kissing Hagar tenderly on the cheek, Abraham sent them into the wilderness of the Northern Sinai.

As Abraham watched mother and son crossing the desert sand, grief pierced his heart. He knew he might never see them again. Reminding himself of the words God had spoken to him concerning Ishmael—*I will make him into a great nation*—Abraham lifted a silent prayer for their safety and prosperity.

May the Lord bless you and keep you, my son! God will keep His promise to you and multiply your descendants. He will surely bless you because you are my son.

Hagar had wandered in the desert before, but Ishmael had never been separated from his father or thrust into an arid wasteland with only the clothes on his back and a little food and water.

He stared at his mother in bewilderment. "Mother, what is happening? Why is Father sending us away?"

The questions stung Hagar's heart.

Glancing back over his shoulder, Ishmael could still see his father standing at the edge of the camp. For fourteen years he had sat at his father's feet listening to the story of how the God of heaven had called Abraham and his relatives out of Ur of the Chaldeans to the land where they now lived. Ishmael had been intrigued to learn that his mother was a gift from the mighty pharaoh of Egypt. Most of all, he loved to hear his father tell him how special he was and that as the firstborn son, he would someday inherit his father's wealth and estate.

But his father had abandoned him, leaving him to wander in this vast desert, cut off from the only home he had ever known. Ishmael was devastated. No longer an heir, he was just the lowly son of a servant woman—a slave.

Ishmael and his mother descended into the looming expanse of the Sinai wilderness. The sun's harsh rays blistered their lips, and sandblasting winds ate at their flesh like locusts. Consumed by the scorching heat, Ishmael collapsed. Hagar frantically squeezed the last drops of water from the goatskin into her son's mouth and then lay him under a small shrub to protect him from the sun.

Stumbling across the sand, Hagar withdrew a stone's throw away. She couldn't bear to watch her only son die. Gut-wrenching sobs escaped her lips as she rocked back and forth, trying to find some measure of comfort in her agony.

Suddenly the cries of her son reached her ears. Ishmael was calling out to his father's God, pleading for the only thing that could sustain his life—water!

The God of heaven heard Ishmael and called out to his distraught mother, "Don't be afraid, Hagar! Go to your son, for I have heard his cries and will make him into a great nation."

When the echoing words faded to silence, Hagar looked around and saw a well nearby. She ran over to fill the goatskin with water and then rushed to Ishmael's side to give him a drink. When he had regained his strength, they continued on their journey until they found a place to settle in the Desert of Paran.

As Ishmael grew into manhood, the God of his father Abraham was with him, and Ishmael sensed that the Lord would keep the promise He had made to his mother in the wilderness.

Someday, Ishmael thought, *God will bless me with descendants as numerous as the desert sand!*

Most of us are familiar with the story of Abraham and Isaac, but how often do we think about Ishmael's role in the story? The Bible doesn't tell us much about the relationship Abraham had with Hagar and Ishmael, but we do know that God promised to bless Ishmael and make him into a great nation. It also seems clear that Abraham loved his son and was distressed at the thought of sending him away (Genesis 21:11). I have a sense that Abraham loved Hagar as well and showed great kindness to her for bearing him a son. Sarah was certainly Abraham's first love, but Hagar was the mother of his firstborn son. That had to count for something!

And yet when Isaac was born, Abraham sent Ishmael and Hagar away. As the years passed and Abraham prepared Isaac to inherit all of his wealth and property, I can't help but wonder if he thought about his firstborn son. I doubt that Abraham forgot about him, but where Ishmael is concerned, the Bible doesn't say much beyond the fact that he had twelve sons: Nebaioth, Kedar, Adbeel, Mibsam, Mishma, Dumah, Massa, Hadad, Tema, Jetur, Naphish, and Kedemah (Genesis 25:12-16).

Before Ishmael died, his sons had settled in the Syro-Arabian Desert near the border of Egypt (verses 13-18). Today Ishmael's descendants comprise many of the Muslim people groups of the Middle East. The great nation God spoke of in the book of Genesis has become the Islamic world of the twenty-first century.

Most Christians in the West think of Abraham as the patriarch of the Jewish people, and by extension, the father of Christianity. But Abraham and his wife, Sarah, were actually descendants of the ancient peoples of Elam in what is now southern Iraq. When God first called Abraham to leave his homeland and journey by faith to a distant land, he and Sarah were living in Ur of the Chaldeans. During Abraham's time, Ur was the agricultural, cultural, and economic center of the known world.[4] The Tigris and Euphrates rivers watered the plains surrounding this ancient city, creating a fertile crescent of lush farmlands and pastures. One of the greatest engineering feats of human civilization, the Tower of Babel, was built by the peoples of ancient Iraq, and the Hanging Gardens of Babylon was among the seven ancient wonders of the world.

The ruins of Ur are located near modern-day Basra, a major seaport on the Persian Gulf, and the holy city of Nasiriyah. Today, Nasiriyah embodies the heart and soul of the Shia sect of the Islamic faith, and yet the people of this region are related to Abraham.

In the days before Abraham, this region was known as Sumer. The Sumerian civilization is said to have developed many scientific, mathematical, and astronomical systems, some of which are still in use today. It is also believed that the first written alphabet came from Sumer.

The Sumerians were known for celestial star worship and astrology. Some of the earliest known pyramids were constructed by moon worshipers in this part of Iraq. A number of these pyramids are even said to predate the famous pyramids of Giza in Cairo, Egypt. Human sacrifices were offered at these sites in idolatrous rituals.

This was Abraham's culture, and yet God called him to leave his family and homeland so that He could establish a personal relationship with the patriarch, setting him apart for a special redemptive purpose. Through this man of faith, God would extend His mercy and grace to all nations, not just the nation of Israel. We may overlook this unique part of Abraham's call, especially if we view God's great plan of salvation through our sometimes narrow Western perspective. It's true that God made a special redeeming covenant with Abraham through Isaac, but if we focus singularly on this aspect of God's plan, we see only a fraction of His heart for the world.

In the Western church, Ishmael is the forgotten son—the son of a slave woman, not the son of the promise. But God didn't forget Ishmael or the promise He made to bless him!

In the twenty-first century, many Muslims in the Middle East and North Africa are stigmatized as abandoned children of God's covenant. Countless numbers of Ishmael's descendants are born into societies that have been separated from God's true family by centuries of Islam, ethnic and religious wars, and extreme poverty. Like Ishmael, many have been driven into a desert of hopelessness to crawl under a bush and die. Squalid deserts like the Gaza Strip and the West Bank, blood-stained regions in Darfur, Sudan, and overcrowded Afghani refugee camps in Pakistan, Jordan, Syria, and Iraq.

In their affliction, the sons and daughters of Ishmael are crying out for help to a God that most of them don't know or understand. But they are calling out to Him nonetheless. Just as the God of Abraham appeared to Hagar and her son in that desert place millennia ago, He is revealing Himself to Ishmael's descendants today, many of whom are longing to know the true God.

God promised Ishmael, "I will make you into a great nation" (Genesis 21:18), and He is fulfilling that promise today as thousands of Muslims are turning to Him through Jesus Christ.

The God of Abraham has not forgotten or forsaken Ishmael's descendants! He loves the Muslim people and longs for them to know Him (2 Peter 3:9). As you'll discover in the pages that follow, God is reaching Ishmael's descendants in miraculous ways, and He is calling the Western church to reach out to them with the good news of His love and grace.

Will we forget the descendants of Ishmael, leaving them to die of thirst in a vast spiritual wilderness, or will we lead them to Jesus, the Spring of Living Water, who is the only One who can quench their thirst?

Ancient Lands
of Abram

Oxus River

Caspian Sea

Persian Gulf

500mi

250

NINEVEH

MESOPOTAMIA

UR

0

MT. ARARAT

ARABIAN
DESERT

Tigris River

HARAN

DAMASCUS

Black Sea

UZ

Red Sea

Mediterranean Sea

MEMPHIS

EGYPT

Nile River

N

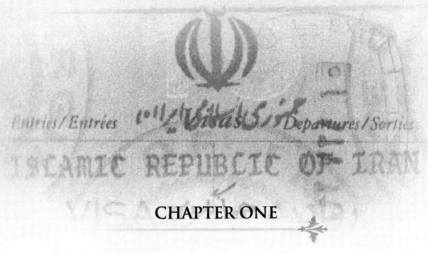

CHAPTER ONE

The Tomb of Imam Ridha

Mashhad, Iran

After months of painstaking preparations and years of prayer, my colleague Phillip and I were finally standing on Iranian soil. The long British Airways flight from London's Heathrow Airport had only fueled our excitement and anticipation. As far as we knew, we were among the first Americans to visit Iran in nearly twenty years.

Relations between Iran and the United States had been hostile ever since fifty-three American hostages were taken captive on November 4, 1979, and held for more than four hundred days at the U.S. embassy in Tehran during the Islamic Revolution. But after a long and bitter hiatus, relations between the two countries had begun to thaw in 1998 as President Clinton and Iran's newly elected president Mohammad Khatami made public overtures toward restoring diplomatic relations.

Now that the United States was seeking to establish a more cordial relationship with Iran, the militant Islamic government had cracked the door open for American visitors. Taking advantage of the warming political climate, Phillip and I jumped at the chance to visit Iran. It would be an adventure few other Americans would experience in a lifetime, and one of my first encounters with Muslims in the Middle East.

Officially we were visiting as tourists, hoping to lay the initial groundwork for bringing Christian tour groups to Iran to explore historic biblical sites around the country. But our tourist visas hadn't been easy to secure. To convince Iranian officials to issue the visas, we had to assure them that we would be visiting several of the country's historic sites. One of the sites on our list was the tomb of Imam Ridha in Mashhad, a city on the remote plains of eastern Iran near the Afghanistan border.

The timing of our visit couldn't have been better. On the day of our tour, more than 130 million Shiite Muslims would be celebrating the Holy Day of Ashura to commemorate the massacre of the prophet Hussein (grandson of the prophet Muhammad) and seventy of his clerics in AD 580. And Imam Ridha's tomb just happened to be located at one of Islam's most sacred sites: the Imam Reza Shrine.

For Shiite Muslims, a pilgrimage to the Reza Shrine is second only to the yearly pilgrimage—or hajj—to Mecca, the pinnacle of religious piety in Islam. As many as twenty million pilgrims flock to the shrine each year to pray and pay their respects at the tomb of Imam Ridha. Seventh in a succession of Shiite holy men, Imam Ridha was martyred in AD 818—a victim of poisoning—and buried in Mashhad, which literally means "a place where martyrs are buried." I had also heard that ever since the miraculous healing of the sultan's son in AD 1150 after he touched the tomb, the sick and disabled throughout the Muslim world came in droves to Imam Ridha's tomb in hopes of being healed.

Soon after our arrival in Tehran, Phillip and I took an early morning flight to Mashhad to tour the sacred shrine. When we stepped off the plane—an old Russian Tupolev jet that comprised most of Iran's domestic air fleet—we spotted a young, black-haired man standing at the bottom of the roll-away metal stairs, holding a small sign that read: Mr. Phillip—Mr. David. This had to be our official Iranian tour guide.

As we approached, the young man smiled in greeting. "Hello! My name is Bakir. Welcome to Mashhad!"

Another young man walked over to a small white car and opened the door.

"This is our driver, Ghazi," Bakir said, escorting us to the waiting car. "We are happy you have come. You will enjoy your time here in Iran, especially in Mashhad."

After loading our bags in the trunk, Ghazi took his seat behind the steering wheel and maneuvered the car toward the exit.

Bakir turned to us with a smile and said, "We will take you first to have tea, and then we will visit the Imam Reza Shrine during the noon prayer time."

Ghazi drove through a maze of dusty streets for several miles and then parked in front of a small shop with bags of tea and spices stacked outside. We followed Bakir into the shop and descended a steep staircase that spiraled down into a cavernous room with vaulted ceilings supported by cracked marble pillars. Several old men were sitting on Persian rugs, silently smoking hookah pipes (glass water pipes used for smoking tobacco). Their dark eyes glanced in our direction as Phillip and I lowered ourselves onto an ornate carpet spread across the floor.

Bakir and Ghazi left us for a few minutes to order cups of hot tea and wafers. Gazing around the smoke-filled room, I noticed several large copper pots in various spots and wondered whether they had some particular use or were merely decorative.

When our hosts returned, we sipped our sweet tea and shared stories about our families. Bakir and Ghazi talked animatedly talked about life in Iran and made us feel very welcome.

Soon Bakir glanced at his watch and said, "It is time to begin our journey to the shrine."

Phillip and I smiled at each other. It was hard to believe, but in less than thirty minutes, we would become two of only a few Westerners to ever visit a sacred Islamic shrine on one of the holiest days of the year for Muslims. I had no idea what to expect, but I had a feeling it would be an experience I'd never forget!

As we drove through the crowded streets toward the Reza Shrine, taxis cut in front of us, honking their horns and then screeching to a halt as the traffic slowed abruptly. How any driver could maneuver in such a crush of vehicles was beyond me, but in the Middle East, it was a matter of survival. Maneuvering through the chaotic Iranian streets made driving in the States seem docile in comparison, but our driver handled the car with ease.

Knowing from experience that it was best not to pay much attention to the hazardous driving conditions, I gazed out the window at little roadside shops, closed for the observance of Ashura. Women cloaked in black from head to toe hurried along the streets with children in tow. Old men congregated on street corners, smoking and observing life happening around them.

During the ride across town, Bakir fulfilled his duties as our tour guide, pointing out monuments to Iran's war veterans, government buildings, theaters of culture—as well as his favorite restaurants. The pride he felt for his country resonated in his voice.

Looking down the street, I saw two large domes rising into the sky. At the same moment, Bakir gestured toward the domes and said with a huge grin, "That is the shrine of Imam Reza! Is it not a sight to behold?"

I had seen photographs of the shrine in travel magazines and thought it was beautiful, but nothing could compare with seeing it in person. The larger dome was a stunning sapphire blue that took my breath away. The smaller golden dome, illuminated by the brilliant sun, was dazzling. Two golden minarets jutted into the sky nearby. Bakir drew our attention to several other minarets scattered around the shrine—fourteen in all, including the gold minarets that marked the site of Imam Ridha's mausoleum. From these minarets, the Islamic call to prayer blared over loudspeakers five times a day, summoning the faithful throughout Mashhad to come to the mosque out of reverence for Allah.

Large crowds were making their way toward the shrine on foot as our guide slowed the car and searched for a place to park. Phillip and I breathed a sigh of relief when we emerged unscathed from our whirlwind trip through town.

Escorted by our guide, we walked quietly across an expansive concrete courtyard toward a row of arched entryways. White, green, and red gemstones created a tapestry of color on the shrine's outer walls, sparkling like a Persian silk carpet against the sky. Passing under one of the arched entryways, we found ourselves in one of seven courtyards that spread like a maze throughout the shrine. The most elaborate was the central mosque courtyard, with three cascading fountains where worshipers performed their ritual cleansing before prayers.

As we followed the burgeoning crowd toward the central courtyard, Bakir informed us that the shrine also contained several libraries filled with a variety of Islamic writings, ancient scrolls, and copies of the Koran and the Hadith (a collection of sayings and traditions from the prophet Muhammad and other holy men).

Passing through another entryway, we entered the mosque courtyard, where white-bearded old men were gathered around fountains of sparkling water, washing their arms and feet as they readied themselves to enter Allah's presence. Young men stood at a respectful distance, waiting in silent reverence for their turn to prepare for prayers.

Phillip and I positioned ourselves near one of the courtyard walls. We knew that as Westerners we probably stood out in the crowd, but we wanted to remain as inconspicuous as possible, watching the events unfold at a respectful distance.

Bakir was eager to show us the shrine, but he wasn't sure whether Americans were permitted to enter the most sacred part of the shrine, where the tomb of Imam Ridha was located. Phillip and I were the first American tourists he had escorted in Mashhad, and he was worried that the religious authorities might punish him severely if he allowed us to visit the tomb.

At the stroke of noon, the call to prayer echoed from the minarets as the masses filed into the sprawling courtyard for prayer. Pious women, draped from head to toe in traditional black *chadors* quietly entered through a separate archway to the right of the men's entrance. Armed Iranian police stood tensely at entrance, their fingers twitching nervously on their Kalashnikov automatic rifles. Their presence assured the crowd that no terrorist would settle old religious scores that day.

As the prayers began, row after row of men knelt in unison and then bowed with their faces to the ground as the *mullah* (teacher) directed worshipers from an elevated pulpit. The intensity of the moment was electrifying.

When the rise and fall of corporate prayers ended, thousands of frenzied supplicants scrambled to their feet and began rushing in mass toward the golden-domed mausoleum of Imam Ridha, writhing and pulsing in religious fervor. Some young men flailed themselves with chains, causing deep bruises to appear all over their bodies; others cut their foreheads with sharp swords until blood oozed down their faces. As they beat their chests and waved their arms, a passionate chant rose from their lips: "Oh, Hussein! Oh, Hussein!"

The wailing drowned out any chance of making myself heard, so I exchanged a wide-eyed glance with Phillip as we struggled to keep our feet in the press of sweat-sour bodies. What had we gotten ourselves into?

Somehow, in the confusion, we became separated from our

guide. I could see him frantically gesturing to us from the courtyard as we were swept along into the bowels of the mosque by a surging tide of human flesh. Fighting desperately to stay close to Phillip, a wave of panic washed over me. Phillip and I exchanged wild-eyed looks as I prayed that God would get us out of there alive. Here we were, two curious Americans in very real danger of being trampled to death under the feet of faithful Muslims who were straining toward the site where Imam Ridha was entombed.

Crushed against a wall of bodies, I fought for air, gasping as I pushed myself up on my toes in a futile effort to see over the crowd. Claustrophobia enveloped me in a suffocating grip, and I wondered how much more I could take before I lost my mind.

Finally the interminable squeezing reached a pinch point, and the crowd spilled out into a huge room that held the imam's tomb. With the shrine now in view, a new surge of intensity propelled the mob forward. A young boy, no more than ten or eleven years of age, seemed to float over the top of people, clambering his way to the front of the room.

All around us, worshipers fought to get closer to the tomb, hands clawing the air in desperation. People were weeping and wailing like tormented souls drowning in a dark ocean, reaching out for a single touch of this sacred tomb.

Helpless to fight the flow of the crowd, Phillip and I suddenly found ourselves facing the tomb. Hundreds of hands reached through the protective grillwork surrounding the tomb to touch and caress its ornate surface. Some worshipers tossed money—gifts for healing—through the bars.

The crowd roiled continuously, slowly forcing us away from the tomb as other worshipers took our place. Then the giant tidal wave of humanity that had engulfed us finally began to recede, carrying us through the exit into a tranquil courtyard of fountains and flowers on the opposite side of the shrine. We had narrowly escaped the jaws of death.

I glanced at Phillip, who looked as shaken as I felt at that moment. Running across the courtyard to meet us, concern written on his face, Bakir apologized profusely for what had happened to us. "Praise be to Allah!" he exclaimed. "You are safe! I feared you would be trampled to death, and I would be executed for failing to protect you."

Following Bakir out of the shrine into the fresh air, I took a deep breath and rested my weary eyes on the expansive horizon. I had never been so thankful for open space in my life!

As Ghazi drove us back to the hotel, I tried to process what I had just experienced. On the surface, the frenzied scene at the tomb appeared to be nothing more than thousands of hysterical Muslims going through some meaningless, superstitious ritual. And yet I knew in my heart that it was so much more than empty ritual. The passion and devotion of these worshipers had been too real to shrug off or discount. I couldn't erase the images of people pressing toward the tomb, faces on fire with passionate devotion, thousands of hands desperately reaching out to touch the sacred tomb, souls crying out to know Allah—and yet not finding Him.

I began to question my own devotion to God. I had always considered myself a passionate and devoted follower of Christ, and yet my devotion couldn't compete with the faithful Shiite Muslims I had observed worshiping their God in unrestrained zeal. I suddenly felt ashamed. I had an intimate, personal relationship with the God of the universe that these followers of Islam were grasping for, and yet I felt as if I had been taking that relationship for granted. I had found the very One they were desperately searching for, but somehow I didn't fully realize the priceless treasure I possessed.

I left the Reza Shrine with a deeper appreciation for my relationship with Jesus, but more than that, I had an epiphany that would transform the way I looked at the Muslim world. That day I realized that many Muslims go to extreme measures to please Allah not because they are blindly following the empty requirements of their faith but because they sincerely want to know the living God. They are searching for Him the only way they know how, and God in His unlimited grace is reaching out to them in Christ, just as He reached out to me.

As I pen these words, I am sitting on a little balcony near the Iranian border. More than ten years have passed since my pilgrimage to Imam Ridha's tomb, but as I've reflected on my experience, I've come to realize that regardless of where people live, they are searching for something to believe in, something to be passionate about. We are all reaching out for Someone who will give us hope and deliver us from the despair of life and the guilt of sin.

The frenzied scene at the tomb that day in 1998 is how most Westerners view the Islamic world. It's a world of extreme religious zeal and radical devotion to Allah that seems to border on insanity.

But is this the *only* face of Islam?

Certainly, the radical devotion to Allah is real, but if we are willing to look beneath the surface, we may discover that religious fanaticism is pointing to a deeper spiritual hunger. Many Muslims are longing to know God personally, and Islam is the only way they know to find Him.

The highest expression of a Muslim's devotion to Allah is the yearly hajj, or pilgrimage, to Mecca, the holiest site in Islam. The fifth and final pillar of Islam, the hajj is required of all Muslims at least once in their lifetime. According to some estimates, more than two and a half million Muslims make pilgrimage to Mecca, Saudi Arabia, every year.

To take part in the hajj,[1] pilgrims must purify themselves—enter a state of Ihram—by abstaining from sexual relations, refraining from arguing, fighting, or killing, and giving up shaving as well as the use of products like colognes or perfumed soaps. Many pilgrims take part in the 'umrah, a second pilgrimage that begins about ten kilometers outside the city at the miqat or entry station to Mecca. There they must bathe to purify themselves and put on white garments called ihram. The women must remove their face coverings, and the men must wear seamless clothing.

As they begin their journey into the city, pilgrims recite the Talbiya Du'a: "Here I am at Your service, O Allah, here I am at Your service! You have no partner. Here I am at Your service. All praise and blessing belong to You. All dominion is Yours and You have no partner."

All the way into Mecca, these Muslim pilgrims recite prayers and perform various rituals. When they reach the Masjid al-Haram

Mosque, they perform the *tawaf*, marching seven times around the *Ka'ba*—a large granite cube in the center of the mosque—while they recite prayers. According to the Koran and Islamic tradition, the *Ka'ba* was built by Abraham and his son Ishmael. It is toward this altar that Muslims turn and pray each day, no matter where they are around the world.

As pilgrims walk around the Ka'ba, they touch the Black Stone, a relic forming a cornerstone of the cube, which, according to Islamic tradition, fell from heaven and revealed to Adam and Eve where to build an altar to offer sacrifices to God. The altar became the first temple on earth.

Muslims believe that the Black Stone was originally dazzling white but has since turned black because of the sins it has absorbed over the years. As pilgrims circle the *Ka'ba*, many stop to kiss the stone as an expression of respect for the prophet Muhammad. After this ritual, pilgrims often take a sip of sacred water—*kam kam*—thought to come from the well God provided for Hagar and Ishmael in the wilderness to keep them from dying of thirst. The *'umrah* ends with the symbolic ritual of walking back and forth seven times between the hills of Safa and Marwa.

Although the hajj incorporates most of the *'umrah* rituals, it also includes trips to several locations outside of Mecca. First is a journey to the town of Mina, where pilgrims spend the night and then depart early the next morning for the valley of Arafat, where they worship God in the midday heat of the open desert, a vivid reminder of hell. The next stop on the hajj is the town of Muzdalifa, where pilgrims gather stones and then return to Mina to throw them at tall pillars, or *jamraat*, to symbolize the stoning of evil and the Devil. Following the throwing of stones, lambs are sacrificed as a ritual offering to Allah, and the meat is given to the poor.

As the days of the hajj draw to a close, pilgrims return to Mecca to march once more around the *Ka'ba*, and then they head back to Mina, where they spend a few more days throwing stones at the pillars.

The final crowning event of the hajj is the *Eid al-Adha*, the feast of sacrifice in which pilgrims commemorate their father Ibrahim's (Abraham's) obedience to Allah when he was commanded to sacrifice his son on an altar. Although the Islamic version of the story portrays Ishmael, rather than Isaac, as the sacrificial lamb, it is actually quite similar to the biblical account. In the end, Allah provided a ram as a substitute for Ishmael, but Abraham's willingness to give up his only son pleased Allah, proving the patriarch's love and devotion.

For Muslims around the world today, elaborate religious rituals and observances are the only ways they know to reach out to God.[2] Allah can only be appeased by works, and the extreme lengths that millions of Muslims go through each year to attain this goal testifies to their sincere desire to know God, however misguided their search.

Islam offers hope to thousands of Muslims who worship at Mecca and Ridha's tomb every year, but most of these pilgrims have never heard about the true God. They have no idea that the God they seek with such sincerity and passion is freely accessible to them in the person of His one and only Son. These are the Muslims I've dedicated my life to reaching with the gospel of the true Prophet of God—Jesus.

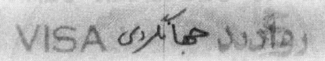

David in Iran

Persian coppersmith in market

CHAPTER TWO

Special Ops In Tehran

Tehran, Iran

The narrow stone street disappeared into one of countless crowded alleys in eastern Istanbul, Turkey, as a small building that housed the official Iranian consulate came into view. I slipped through the front door and made my way down the hallway to the consulate office.

When I entered the cramped waiting room, furnished with only a few chairs, I was immediately the center of attention. Women dressed in solid black from head to toe scrutinized me suspiciously from behind their veils, while young men in Levi's and T-shirts gave me curious looks. I stood awkwardly by the door, trying not to look too conspicuous.

It seemed an eternity before the next window opened up. I walked to the counter and slid my blue American passport into the metal tray under the glass barrier. A young lady behind the glass looked straight at me, her piercing olive eyes the only feature visible through the narrow slit in her black veil. Her laserlike eyes, although pleasant, seemed to penetrate my soul, asking why an American would want to visit her country—the Islamic Republic of Iran. She glanced down at my passport, folded it, and then slowly rose from her desk and disappeared into the back of the consulate office—with my passport in hand.

Less than a year had passed since my colleague Phillip and I had visited Iran as tourists. It had been my first trip to Iran, and my first up-close encounter with Muslims from the Middle East. I had always wanted to explore this ancient biblical land, and my visit in May had been a dream come true. Phillip and I had toured a number of historical sites across Iran on that trip, but now we had a special mission to carry out. A trip of eternal significance.

The young lady from the Iranian consulate eventually returned with a middle-aged gentleman dressed in a navy blue suit and tie. With a polite smile and an extended hand, he greeted me. "I see this is your second visit to Iran. We are happy Americans want to visit our country! We have waited for you many years. You and your friend are the first Americans we have processed visas for at this office. We will remember you today. You are most welcome."

Taking my passport, I thanked the man and then turned to leave. Outside the consulate, I quickly flipped through the passport to the page bearing a huge official stamp in black ink for the Islamic Republic of Iran. The stamp, in both English and Persian, covered the entire page. It was hard to believe I'd been granted a second opportunity to visit one of the most ancient and mysterious civilizations on earth—and the most misunderstood.

The next day, Phillip and I boarded a Boeing 747 destined for Iran. Our visit just happened to coincide with the sacred Islamic holiday of Ramadan, a month of ritual fasting and purification. Every seat on the plane was packed with Iranians returning home from Istanbul and other exotic locations. Well-to-do businessmen wore fine-tailored silk suits, likely purchased in Istanbul's Old City bazaar. Iranian women, testing the limits of *sharia* law—the social and religious code of Islam, based on the Koran—pushed their bright-colored headscarves as far back on their foreheads as they dared, revealing the newest hair colors and makeup from L'Oréal. Gucci jeans and fine perfume from Paris added fuel to the fire, as the airborne fashion show started, Persian style. Children sat contently in their seats, eating sweets and playing with stuffed Mickey Mouse dolls.

As fate would have it, Phillip and I were seated in the very front section of the plane. We were the only foreigners on the flight! Everyone did a double take as they passed by, their expressions silently asking, "Did these guys board the wrong plane?"

The flight attendants brought us copies of the *International Herald Tribune* in English and Farsi. Phillip and I looked at each other and smiled. Only in the Middle East!

It seemed we would never get off the ground, but eventually the 747 taxied and then climbed slowly skyward. As I peered out the porthole window, the bleak mountainous deserts of Turkey and central Iraq blended with the brilliant reds and purples of sunset on the western horizon. Gazing eastward into the approaching night, I pondered what awaited us. Would Phillip and I pull off our secret mission in Iran without being arrested? *Only by the grace of God!* I mused as I breathed a prayer for protection.

My mind raced with countless scenarios over the next two hours of flight time. Finally our plane began its descent through the night sky toward the Imam Khomeini International Airport. Women readjusted their headscarves to conceal more hair; some covered their entire bodies in traditional black *chadors*.

Puffs of blue smoke from the plane's wheels vaporized into the cool desert air as our modern-day camel touched down on the tarmac. I could hear passengers in the back clapping their hands, while others broke out into high-pitched, ululating Middle Eastern vocalizations—*lalalalalalal!* Over the intercom, a pleasant female voice welcomed passengers to Tehran in English and Farsi.

After we disembarked, Phillip and I were shepherded toward a passport-and-customs line for inspection. The eyes peering from behind a black veil this time were not as pleasant as the young woman's at the Iranian consulate in Istanbul. I knew I might be the first American this female security officer had ever met. Or perhaps she had already met other Americans and had formed an unfavorable impression of them. I would never know.

After a stern look at me and my passport, the woman firmly stamped my visa and motioned me to pass through the gate. Phillip and I headed for the baggage-claim area to retrieve our luggage. The area looked more like a merchant's bazaar than a place to collect luggage. Slowly making their circuit on the conveyor belt were rolls of textiles and carpets from Turkey, tea sets, copper pans, wood carvings, and suitcases packed with everything from spices and frankincense to Gucci perfume and Levi's 501 jeans. I, too, had brought precious goods with me from Turkey: Bibles in Arabic and Farsi, two seventy-pound suitcases full of them!

Collecting my bags, I proceeded with the rest of the crowd to the last security checkpoint. Another female security officer scrutinized me from behind a black veil. We made eye contact, and I tried desperately not to show any strain as I lifted one of my suitcases and slammed it down on the conveyor belt in front of me. The suitcase quickly disappeared into the cavernous darkness of an antiquated screening machine.

I closed my eyes and inhaled deeply, silently lifting a simple request to God: "In the Bible You healed blind people so they could see. This is one time I'm asking You to blind someone so that others might see. Lord, You know the believers here desperately need these Bibles. Please get them through this checkpoint safely."

Holding my breath, I slowly walked through the metal detector. No alarm sounded. No armed guards confronted me. Emerging safely on the other side, I let out a ragged breath. It seemed like an eternity before the edge of my suitcase slowly appeared at the other end of the screening machine. Suddenly, the conveyor belt stopped and then went into reverse, sucking my suitcase back into the jaws of the machine. The security official's forehead wrinkled and her eyes narrowed as she squinted at the computer screen.

My mind began to race. I swallowed hard, heart pounding, palms sweating, knees shaking. Dark images flooded my brain—blindfolded Americans on CNN, paraded in front of thousands of screaming

Islamic fundamentalists chanting, "Death to the Americans!"

"What is in the suitcase?" the lady asked in a perfect British accent.

Recovering from the initial shock, I mumbled, "They're books for my friends here in Tehran. It's Ramadan…you know, a time for gifts. They're gifts."

Tilting her head, she nodded; then with a slight smile and wave of her hand, she allowed my suitcases through. "Welcome to Iran. It is nice of you to bring such gifts for our people."

Moments later, I stood alone with my two suitcases of Bibles on the other side of passport control, waiting for Phillip to join me. He was enduring the same scrutiny I had just survived, only at a different security checkpoint.

When I spotted him emerging from the baggage-screening line, I smiled and waved. We had made it through customs in one piece, and no one had discovered our precious cargo. God had performed a miracle before our very eyes!

We strolled out of customs into the main terminal, where two gentlemen from Iran's Ministry of Tourism met us.

"Hello, Mr. Phillip and Mr. David," they warmly greeted us. "Welcome to Iran! We are happy to have you here!"

The Iranian government had assigned Abu and Marsan to escort us during our visit to make sure we saw all the hot tourist attractions in the capital city and throughout the country. They had also been assigned to monitor our activities to make sure we didn't get into any trouble—or turn out to be spies. After all, this was still Iran, and we were Americans.

Abu and Marsan led us out of the airport to a little white van parked nearby. They loaded our luggage in the back compartment and then shuttled us to our hotel in downtown Tehran, where we would spend the next few days. The former Sheraton—now the Homa Hotel—had seen better days during the Shah's reign, before its glory faded following the Islamic Revolution in the late 1970s. Even so, the guests sitting in the lobby looked prosperous, and I could hear them chatting in German, French, and Arabic as they sipped on sweet coffee and browsed through Western and Iranian newspapers. Kodak film and gold jewelry from Dubai were prominently displayed in all the shops.

Abu introduced us to the desk clerk and made sure our accommodations were set; then he and Marsan escorted us to our rooms. By now it was one o'clock Friday morning—the Muslim holy day of prayer. We quickly unpacked our pajamas, brushed our teeth, and collapsed into our beds. As I nodded off, I thought about the adventure that awaited us the following day.

Just before first light the next morning—at 5:28, to be exact—the droning call to prayer (the adhan) blared from the minarets of local mosques, jarring Phillip and me from our jet-lagged slumber. There was no need for an alarm clock! As I lay there listening to the rising and falling tones of *"Allahu akbar! Allahu akbar!"* it sounded as if the *muezzin* (reciter) was still slumbering.

Slowly, the summons grew in intensity, and the entire landscape of Tehran seemed to vibrate with the shrill call to the faithful, reminding them of their obligation to honor Allah and His prophet Muhammad. For the citizens of Iran, there was no escaping the call. Islam pervaded culture, society, education, the everyday life of the people.

I didn't feel very faithful as I groped for the light switch in the dark. When I pulled back the drapes, my crusty eyes recoiled from the early morning sun rising in the east. Before me lay the sprawling city of Tehran like a slumbering lion. The dusty, bustling streets from the night before were silent and empty on this day of prayer. Shops would be closed until sunset, and the heavy traffic that normally clogged the narrow streets of Tehran would be lighter than usual.

Phillip and I had arranged to meet Abu and Marsan for breakfast downstairs in the hotel lobby before touring several historic and religious sites throughout the city, as well as visiting a local travel agency owned and operated by an Armenian Christian. At the agency, we would discuss bringing Christian groups to Iran to explore historic biblical sites around the country, our official reason for visiting Iran. We had laid the initial groundwork for the tours in May and were hoping to finalize the details on this trip.

After finishing our business at the travel agency, we would return to the hotel for a time of rest and a free evening, at least until the officials from the Ministry of Tourism left. After that, we had other plans.

The morning was so packed with activity, it flew by at lightning speed, and by the time we returned to the hotel, my eyelids were closing as if sacks of flour were weighing them down. But sleep had to wait. As soon as Abu and Marsan left us early in the afternoon, I headed downstairs to partake in God's gift to missionaries, a cup of Middle Eastern Christian crank—strong coffee in a tiny cup. I knew not to drink to the very bottom of the cup. Any naive soul who did would get a mouthful of sludge like a triple shot of espresso from Starbucks. A real eye opener!

After my afternoon java fix, energized and alert, I went back upstairs to our room, where Phillip and I reviewed our plans and prepared to deliver our priceless cargo from abroad. In a couple of hours, we would leave our hotel and embark on a "special ops" mission with eternal consequences. We were headed to a Friday-night prayer service at a church several miles from our hotel. There, a handful of underground church leaders would meet us to receive the desperately needed Bibles and study materials we had brought.

We had heard about these courageous believers before, but that evening would be our first opportunity to actually meet and worship with them in a church setting. We were excited—and apprehensive. We hadn't forgotten that we were Americans in Iran.

Not knowing whether we would be watched or followed after leaving the hotel, we mapped out a route that would first get us near the University of Tehran. Then we would walk separately to the church, which was several blocks away, so that one of us could keep watch over the other to ensure that we both arrived safely at our destination. The risks of being pursued by the authorities were very real, and if we ended up getting arrested, we didn't want to implicate the church leaders.

Opening the suitcases we had brought, we began to repack the bulky study Bibles, transferring them into large backpacks we would wear to the church. Loaded with Bibles and a few pieces of clothing to conceal them, our packs bulged like sacks of potatoes.

When late afternoon arrived, Phillip and I slipped unnoticed out of the hotel lobby and strolled casually down the street to hail a cab. The streets were strangely quiet, with very few cars traveling along them. Since it was Ramadan, most people were observing the daily fast until after sunset. We hadn't factored this into our plans, and the thought of roaming the streets of Tehran without blending into the crowds only increased our anxiety.

It seemed surreal walking down the ancient streets of this Persian capitol, carrying backpacks full of Bibles and looking for a Christian church we didn't even know how to get to. We had a business card with the address of Tehran University scribbled on it, but we had no idea where the campus and the church actually were.

Standing conspicuously on the street corner near our hotel, we waited for a taxi. Unable to speak Farsi, we prayed we would find a university student who spoke English. All of a sudden, like a scene from *American Graffiti*, a vintage 1957 Chevrolet appeared out of nowhere, swerved over to the curb, and screeched to a stop in front of us.

A potbellied, middle-aged man jumped out and, with a huge smile on his face, said, "Taxi?"

No university student; not even a bonafide taxi driver. But the man spoke intelligible English, even though it was a bit rough.

"My name Nabeel!" he said as he grabbed our backpacks and tossed them in his trunk. Phillip and I scrambled to get into the Chevy; then Nabeel sped away down the vacant street.

Reluctantly I handed him the business card with the address to the university written in Farsi. Nodding his head in acknowledgment, Nabeel floored the accelerator as he turned and blurted out, "Europeans? Teachers? University professors?"

Phillip and I laughed. "No. Americans… Travel agents."

Nabeel's face lit up. "You know Clinton? He and Khatami friends. I like America. Bruce Willis…football…Chevrolet…my car. Good!"

No…bad!

Nabeel's Chevy sailed down the streets of Tehran as paranoia invaded my mind. I imagined every conceivable worst-case scenario… Nabeel would get stopped for speeding. The police would discover two Americans in the car and would ask us where we were going. Then they would search Nabeel's trunk and open our backpacks. Bingo! Bibles! Busted! We would then be kicked out of the country and our Bibles confiscated.

Or events could take a darker, more sinister turn. Was the portly cab driver a setup, sent to pick us up so we could be tailed by the religious police? Could someone at the hotel, or even our tour guides, have tipped off the police that we left the hotel on unofficial business? I thought about the man at the consulate in Istanbul, who said he would remember our names. Had we been watched all this time? Or maybe the customs lady at the airport had purposely let the Bibles through so the police could track us to the church and arrest us along with the other believers. I was overwhelmed with doubt.

I grabbed Nabeel's shoulder, shouting at him to stop the car and let us out. Startled, he didn't seem to understand at first, but then he caught on. Abruptly steering the old Chevy to the side of the road, Nabeel maneuvered it to a sliding stop. We were still several blocks from the university.

Rattled and still paranoid, I grabbed my backpack out of Nabeel's trunk and then slipped him a hundred thousand rial note (the equivalent of fifteen U.S. dollars). Nabeel smiled and waved as he got into his ancient Chevy and then roared off down the street.

I stared after him for a moment, wondering whether I'd made a mistake. Phillip and I glanced at each other and then started walking down the sidewalk toward the university. Along the way, a familiar sight greeted us: the former U.S. embassy compound, the site of the 1979 hostage crisis.

The moment was surreal. The embassy eagle—the seal on the huge metal gates that opened to the compound—still bore the distinct marks of a goat head with horns, symbolizing America as the Great Satan. Ironically, the compound had been turned into a hospital for Iranian military veterans wounded in the Iran-Iraq war.

An armed Iranian soldier stood at the entrance, his eyes warily following us as we passed by. Across the street, a fifteen-story building had been painted from top to bottom like an American flag. At the bottom end of each red and white stripe, a black bomb pointed downward as if dropped from an airplane. The blue square was filled with white skulls instead of stars. Stenciled across the entire breadth of the flag were the words "Down with the USA" in bold black letters. A chill shot up my spine, but we continued on. We were on a mission; the Bibles had to get to the church.

As early evening settled over the city, hundreds of Shiite Muslims were coming out of the main downtown mosque after evening prayers. No rioting or chants of "Death to America!" No American flags burning in the streets or effigies of Bill Clinton hanging from poles. Everyone looked calm and peaceful. Yet the police were on every corner, watching intently in every direction.

Phillip and I pressed on, trying not to make eye contact with anyone, especially the police. I imagined that we had neon lights flashing over our heads: "We're Americans! Stop us! We're carrying Bibles in these bulging backpacks!"

When we arrived at the university, we paused for a few moments to catch our breath. I glanced around at students and families enjoying the parklike atmosphere. Life seemed very normal.

Suddenly I realized that people were staring at us curiously. Our cover had been blown. They knew we weren't Persian. That was our cue to separate and begin the final leg of our journey to the church. I looked around as casually as possible to see if the police or other government officials were heading in our direction. We seemed to be in the clear—at least for the moment.

We had decided that Phillip would make his way down the street first as I kept watch, scanning the area for any potential threats. As soon as he stopped, I followed while he kept watch. In this way, we slowly made progress toward our final destination.

Finally we spotted the church. After our anxious trek through the streets of Tehran, we slipped into the back of the building as worshipers were gathering for the Friday-night service. I was stunned to see so many Christians—easily a couple thousand people—worshiping openly in an Islamic regime like Iran.

Phillip and I stood uncertainly at the church entrance and glanced around the sanctuary. We needed to speak with the pastor, whoever he was.

A young man at the door looked mildly shocked to see two foreigners standing in front of him. He questioned us extensively, taking great care not to reveal the pastor's identity to strangers off the street. Iranian intelligence had been known to plant agents in the Christian churches to monitor members' activities and arrest those who had converted from Islam to Christianity. Yet it was obvious we weren't spies—at least not for the Iranian government.

After a few awkward moments, the young man went away and then returned with a middle-aged man wearing a suit and tie. With an apprehensive look on his face, the older man asked what our business was and who had sent us.

"Brother Mark sent us," I ventured, hoping he would recognize the name.

Immediately, the man broke into a wide smile. "Welcome my friends. We have been expecting you! Come, have tea in my office."

We had found the pastor.

Entering a simply furnished room off to the side of the sanctuary, Phillip and I delivered our precious cargo of Bibles. Our mission to Iran had been accomplished! Opening my backpack, I handed the pastor one of the Bibles. His face beamed with joy as he took the Bible in his hands.

"These are so precious!" he told us. "So many of our people need God's Word to help them grow in their faith. Many want to teach others about God. These study Bibles are an answer to our prayers for the church in Iran! On behalf of our people, thank you for this gift you have given us!"

After enjoying tea and cookies, we left the pastor's office and climbed the stairs leading to a balcony that overlooked the main sanctuary. The service had already begun, and songs of praise filled the sanctuary as Iranian believers lifted their voices to God in Farsi. The worship swelled for more than an hour, and then the pastor gave an encouraging message from the Scriptures.

Three hours later, the service came to an end. I could have stayed for several more hours, soaking up the worship with believers a world away from America, whose lives radiated the love of Jesus. I felt a kinship with these brothers and sisters in Christ, even though their language and culture was radically different from mine.

After praying with the pastor and several other church leaders, Phillip and I said our good-byes and stepped back out into the streets of Tehran, bustling now with activity. Another day of fasting had ended for Muslims, and the somber-faced worship I'd noticed earlier in the day had transformed to ecstatic celebration.

That night, Phillip and I joined with more than two thousand Persian-Iranians, worshiping God with a love and passion not often seen in the West. In spite of great persecution and death threats from Islamic leaders and a repressive government, many Iranians are coming to faith in Christ. But to grow strong in their faith, they need the nourishing food of God's Word.

The risks Phillip and I took to deliver our small stash of Bibles to a group of believers in Tehran could never compare with the dangers Middle Eastern converts face every day as they seek to follow Christ. The people of Iran are hungry for God's Word in their own language. And God is meeting that need in some amazing ways. Even through American tourists!

As Western Christians, we may find it hard to believe that a growing number of Iranians are becoming brothers and sisters in Christ. Surprising as this is to us, it's no surprise to God. The people of Iran (formerly known as Persia) are close to His heart!

In ancient times, the people of this region were referred to as

Parthians (Acts 2:9). They were skilled artisans, gifted in weaving, metalwork, and jewelry making. The Parthians also practiced the ancient religions of Mithraism and Zoroastrianism.

The Parthian Empire stretched between the Caspian Sea and the Persian Gulf and at its height, between 247 BC and AD 228, controlled the Silk Road, the main trade route that extended from China to the Mediterranean Sea. The Parthians also conquered most of the Middle East, including areas of present-day Turkey, Armenia, Azerbaijan, Turkmenistan, Afghanistan, Pakistan, Syria, Lebanon, and Palestine.

The Bible first mentions the kingdom of Persia in the Old Testament book of Esther. A young Jewish orphan girl named Hadassah (Esther) was taken into the harem of the Persian king Xerxes and became one of his wives. In her elevated position as queen, Esther pleaded with the king for the lives of her people—the Jews—saving them from extermination. Afterward, many Persians throughout the empire—127 provinces in all, from India to Ethiopia—began to worship Esther's God.

Centuries later, the descendants of the same Persians who worshiped Jehovah during King Xerxes' reign traveled to Jerusalem for the Jewish Feast of Pentecost. When they arrived in the holy city, they heard murmurings about a man named Jesus who had been crucified by the Romans for claiming to be God's Son, the Messiah or Anointed One.

As the Persians were pondering this news, they heard strange rumors about this man's disciples. Word had spread that these men were on the streets of Jerusalem, praising God in languages of other lands. Wanting to see this event for themselves, the Persians made their way to the house where Jesus' disciples were staying. There, they heard a man named Peter declare that God had raised His Son, Jesus, the crucified Savior, from the grave to save all of humanity from the deadly scourge of sin. As the Persians listened to his words, a distant memory returned to them of a time in Persia when God raised up Queen Esther to redeem her people from certain death. Now these Persians worshipers of the true God were hearing about Jesus, Jewish Messiah, who was their Messiah too.

Today, in spite of the barriers of fear, disdain, and distrust that exist between Iran and the West, the good news is that the Persian people are welcoming the Messiah into their hearts. According to the Joshua Fund, when Ayatollah Khomeini led the Islamic Revolution in the late 1970s, there were only about five hundred known Muslim converts to Christianity. Today, based on interviews conducted with more than twenty Iranian pastors and church leaders, there are well over one million Shia Muslim converts to Christianity!

Small house churches are meeting all over the country, and established fellowships in Tehran and other major cities are seeing many people come to faith in Jesus Christ. In the face of persecution, harassment, and in some cases death, Persian believers are standing strong in their faith.

God is also working through indigenous believers who are risking their lives to bring God's Word—the Bible—to their people. Among them are three young Kurdish brothers who experienced great hardship during the eight-year Iran-Iraq war in the 1980s. The war exacted an enormous toll on these men and their family. During this time, their father became very ill and eventually died. But rather than taking up arms and fighting to avenge their father's death, these young men were determined to make an eternal difference in the lives of their people.

Facing extreme dangers, they journeyed with a team of donkeys along ancient nomadic trade routes, through the remote mountain passes and rugged canyons of Western Iran, which are often infiltrated by al-Qaida fighters. The mission of these three brothers? To deliver Bibles and other Christian literature in Farsi and Arabic to small Kurdish-Christian house churches.

Because of their courage and the precious cargo they have delivered to remote parts of their country, Iranian and Kurdish believers are growing in their faith as they learn more about their Messiah through His Word.

Dark storm clouds may hang over this ancient land, but on the backs of donkeys—and even in tourists' backpacks—God's Word is reaching the people of Iran. God loves the Persian people, and He is accomplishing His purpose for their lives!

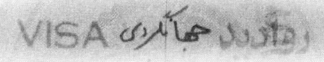

U.S. Embassy - Tehran, Iran

Prophetic graffiti

CHAPTER THREE

Amir's Strange Encounter

Baghdad, Iraq

Amir was a prominent member of the infamous Baath Party in Iraq and had served as a colonel in Saddam Hussein's armed forces for many years. As an officer in the elite Republican Guard during the bloody Iran-Iraq War in the 1980s, Amir received many medals and promotions for his faithful and heroic military service. One of the rewards of service also included a nice home in an affluent Sunni Muslim neighborhood of Baghdad. Amir's family life was materially secure, and the future seemed bright. Yet Amir had very little peace in his heart.

Every day, he prayed faithfully to Allah, prostrating himself on his prayer rug at home and at work, saying all the right words. He fasted, gave alms to the poor, and went to the mosque every Friday with all the other devout Muslims in his neighborhood. He kept all the traditions of his faith and considered himself a good Muslim. And yet Allah seemed so far away, so impersonal.

Again and again Amir cried out in prayer, asking Allah to become real to him. But heaven remained silent. A vast emptiness engulfed Amir's heart.

One day in October of 2002, Amir walked to his home through the streets of Baghdad as he had done hundreds of times before. The air hung heavily over the city as the rumblings of war echoed in the distance. Iraqi intelligence had confirmed that a coalition of American and European forces would soon attack Baghdad in an intensive effort to remove Saddam Hussein from power. The entire Iraqi army was on high alert, anticipating the moment they would be called upon to defend their city. Troops and armaments were being strategically repositioned all over the country as the military prepared for the all-but-certain invasion of coalition forces.

More than a month had passed since anyone had seen Saddam Hussein in public. Although they were loyal to their leader, many soldiers in Saddam's ranks were worried about what he might do in the weeks leading up to the invasion. Most feared for the safety of their families.

Amir's thoughts were consumed with all these concerns as he walked along the busy streets of Baghdad that afternoon. Suddenly he froze in his tracks and grabbed his chest. Breathing heavily, sweat beading on his forehead, he began to panic. What would happen to him and his family? What would become of his people, his country, and the dictator who had ruled Iraq with an iron fist since 1979?

Saddam's sins were well documented, his brutal treatment of anyone who opposed him, especially the Shiites and the Kurds, who had suffered immensely under Saddam's rule. Abu Ghraib—the notorious prison where thousands of Iraqis had been subjected to deplorable living conditions, unimaginable torture, and eventual execution—and the Anfal Campaign against the Kurds in the late 1980s were just two horrors of the past that had been bubbling under the surface and were now ready to spew forth like a raging volcano.

If Saddam fell from power, it would be only a matter of time before blood would flow in the streets as the Kurds and Shiites sought retribution for the countless atrocities of Saddam's regime. The clock was ticking. Amir could hear the rattling of sabers in his head. He was terrified of what would happen once war had unleashed a tidal wave of ethnic violence against the Sunni population. What would he and his family do? Where could they flee?

Baghdad's streets were bustling with activity that afternoon. Pushing his way through the crowds, Amir staggered around a corner onto the street where his family lived. A moment later, a kind-looking man with a pleasant smile approached him and grasped his hand.

"Don't be afraid," the stranger said. "God has heard you. Take heart!" He placed a book in Amir's hand and then disappeared into the crowd.

Amir's eyes grew wide when he realized that the book was an Arabic Bible. Startled, he looked around to see if anyone had witnessed the transaction. Relieved that no one seemed to have noticed, Amir quickly slipped the Bible under his jacket and hurried home. He decided it was best to keep his encounter with the stranger a secret from his family and friends.

Curious about the book in his possession, Amir began to read it every day. As he discovered the true and living God in the pages of the Bible, his heart came alive. His anxiety about the future vanished, and a sense of wholeness and peace filled the emptiness in his heart. Allah no longer felt distant and unapproachable. He was real, and He was revealing Himself to Amir. Allah had finally answered Amir's pleas and prayers!

In the New Testament, Amir read that God loved him and sent His Son, Jesus, to die for Amir's sins—even the sins of the whole world! Through the words of Jesus, Amir realized that he needed to be born again to see God's kingdom. So in a simple act of humility, he spread out his prayer rug—the same one he used for his daily Islamic prayers—bowed with his forehead to the ground, and asked Jesus to give him a new birth. In that moment of surrender, Amir came fully alive to God.

Amir desperately wanted to share this life-changing experience with his wife and children, but the fear of their rejection gripped him. *My wife will think the stress I'm under has driven me mad,* he thought.

Amir continued to read his Bible in secret, and in place of his daily *namaz* (Islamic prayers), he prayed to Jesus. On the surface, he looked like the faithful Muslim he had always been, going through all the usual postures and rituals of prayer. But during these times, Amir began to ask that God would reveal Himself to his wife and children in the same miraculous way He had revealed Himself to Amir.

As the threat of war closed in, and Iraq spiraled into chaos, Amir radiated God's peace.

Amir's daughter Miriam had no idea what had happened to her father. His behavior had changed radically over the past few months. He used to return home from work full of hatred and sharp words, but now he was patient and loving, so calm and peaceful that he almost seemed reborn.

Miriam had grown up with her three younger siblings in a very strict Sunni Muslim family. She had followed all of the religious practices and traditions of the Islamic faith since childhood. But now at the age of nineteen, she was confused about the changes she was seeing in her father. She and her mother, Hadassah, often wondered what was wrong with him. Her mother had even begun to pray over him and write verses from the Koran on little slips of paper that she hung around her neck to ward off the evil spirits she thought were oppressing him.

Then one day, Miriam found her mother in the kitchen, sobbing uncontrollably. At first Miriam thought her father had abandoned the family, but her mother quickly calmed those fears.

When Miriam asked what was troubling her mother, Hadassah blurted out, "I saw a man in a brilliant white robe standing at the foot of my bed during the night. He claimed that He was God and that I should worship Him!"

As Miriam ran downstairs to get her father, her confusion deepened. Her father had become such a different man over the past year, and now her mother was having visions of men in white robes claiming to be God. Were her parents going crazy? Had the foreign infidels brought an evil jinn (spirit) with them to afflict the people of Iraq?

Falling into her father's arms, Miriam began to weep as she told him about her mother's vision. By the time they ran upstairs to the kitchen, the other children had already gathered to see what the commotion was all about. Miriam looked frantically from her mother to her father, unsure of what to do. Then she noticed a strange gleam in her father's eyes. Suddenly he rushed over to the family and pulled them into his arms, weeping openly as he shared his newfound faith in Jesus Christ. With cries of joy, he invited each of them to accept Jesus into their hearts.

Miriam looked at her father in stunned silence. She couldn't believe what she had just heard! A nightmare was unfolding before her very eyes, and yet she sensed hope growing in her heart. It was as if God Himself had come down from heaven and was standing in their midst. Like a mighty waterfall, God's Spirit washed over Miriam and her entire family. With tears rolling down her cheeks, Miriam opened her heart to Jesus, as did the other members of her family. Finally she understood the miraculous transformation that had taken place in her father's life.

When the Americans attacked Baghdad in March of 2003, Saddam's military forces were quickly subdued. Saddam himself was eventually captured, tried, and hanged for his crimes against humanity. By order of the Coalition Provisional Authority, Saddam's military was completely dismantled, and Amir's position as a colonel in the Iraqi army was eliminated. The elite Republican Guard, who had fought tenaciously until the end, were among the last of Saddam's armed forces to surrender.

Ethnic reprisals came as well. Even the prominent Sunni

neighborhood where Amir and his family lived became a target of Shia Muslims. Some Sunnis lost their homes to religious militias, bandits, and soldiers of fortune. Others lost their lives as rival clans demanded blood for blood to settle family scores that were centuries old.

At first, fear gripped Amir's heart as he helplessly watched his country being ripped apart. Then he remembered the stranger who had given him a Bible and told him not to be afraid. Peace flooded Amir's heart. He was now a child of a loving God, and he didn't need to worry or fear. The same God who had given him and his family new life in Christ would also take care of them and provide for their needs. Amir was confident he could trust God for their future.

Neighbors and friends became aware that Amir and his family had converted to Christianity, and soon the family began experiencing religious persecution from fundamentalist Sunni and Shia communities. The persecution became so severe that Amir and his family were forced to leave all their earthly possessions behind and evacuate to a safer area of Baghdad on the west side of the Tigris River. There they found a community of Christians who took them in and provided them with a simple shelter.

Amir and Hadassah were deeply grateful to God for leading them to this compassionate group of believers, who encouraged them to continue on in their walk with God. In spite of all the hardships their family endured, Amir and Hadassah never lost their joy and love for God.

Today, Amir and his family continue to grow in their faith and rejoice that they have been counted worthy to suffer for Jesus Christ. They are excited to share God's love for the Muslim world, and they now attend one of the fastest growing Christian fellowships in Baghdad.

As the security situation has improved, Amir and Hadassah have returned to the Sunni and Shia neighborhoods they were driven from after the war to share the love and hope of God that enabled them to survive their darkest hours. They are still considered Sunni Muslims, since it's illegal to change one's national identity or religious heritage in Iraq. And yet their Sunni background is the passport they need to gain access to Muslim neighborhoods in Baghdad so they can reach out to their fellow Iraqis with God's love.

As Amir and Hadassah meet the everyday needs of Muslim families through the distribution of food-aid packages and medical supplies, God is opening doors for them to share their newfound faith in Christ with their people. Ironically, those who once persecuted Amir and his family are now the ones who seem most open to hearing the gospel.

Just as God revealed Himself to Amir and Hadassah, He is reaching out in miraculous ways to a growing number of Sunni and Shia Muslims throughout Iraq!

I first met Amir, Hadassah, and their daughter Miriam at a prayer conference in 2008 on the Iraq-Iran border. Miriam was beaming from ear to ear, her face radiating God's love and joy. When I heard their story, I was deeply moved as I realized that nothing can hinder God from touching lives and changing hearts, even the heart of one of Saddam Hussein's highest-ranking former military officers!

Hadassah's experience illustrates that even today God is calling Muslims to faith in Him through dreams and visions. In fact, God has spoken to people in the Middle East this way for millennia. During Bible times, angelic appearances, visions, and dreams were commonplace, exerting a tremendous influence over people's lives. Often involving matters of life and death, dreams were taken very seriously.

Dreams are abundant throughout the Bible, particularly in the Old Testament. In the book of Genesis, Joseph dreamed that one day his entire family would bow down to him. Little did he realize that God would fulfill this dream years later in Egypt when Joseph's brothers bowed down before him in submission, completely unaware that Pharaoh's chief administrator was the brother they had sold to a passing caravan a lifetime ago in Canaan. (See Genesis 37 and 42.)

God also blessed Joseph with the ability to interpret dreams. When Pharaoh's dreams disturbed him, he sent for Joseph to find out what they meant. Years earlier, Joseph had correctly interpreted the prophetic dreams of Pharaoh's cupbearer and chief baker. Three days after Joseph told each man the meaning of his dream, the chief baker was hanged, and the cupbearer's life was spared.

Pharaoh heard about Joseph's gift for interpreting dreams and summoned him to explain the meaning of his dream. When Pharaoh told Joseph the dream, God revealed to Joseph that a devastating famine would soon occur throughout the land, and he advised the king of Egypt to store away as much grain as possible during the years of abundance. Pharaoh was so pleased with Joseph's interpretation and advice that he appointed him chief administrator of Egypt. (See Genesis 40–41.)

Fewer dreams are recorded in the New Testament. Perhaps the most familiar example is the dream in which God warned Joseph to flee with Mary and their child to Egypt because King Herod was determined to kill Jesus. When the king died, God appeared to Joseph again in a dream, telling him that it was safe to return to Israel (Matthew 2:13-20).

Just as dreams abound in the Bible, accounts of angelic encounters occur frequently as well. Angels intervened in human affairs, such as the three strangers who appeared to Abraham's nephew Lot and warned him that Sodom was about to be destroyed (Genesis 19). Angels also announced special events that would take place, such as the birth and resurrection of Jesus, and the births of other people, such as Samson and John the Baptist, whom God would use in powerful ways.

Unlike dreams and angelic encounters, visions were rare in Bible times. During most of Israel's history, the people strayed from the Lord and engaged in such wicked behavior that He turned His face away from them. This could be one reason God appeared so seldom to people in visions.

In 1 Samuel 3:1, we read that in the days when Eli and his wicked sons were priests in Israel, "the word of the LORD was rare [and] there were not many visions." This suggests that the people's sins may have prevented them from experiencing God in this powerful way. And yet God appeared to young Samuel repeatedly in a vision, calling out his name. Samuel mistakenly thought that his master Eli was summoning him, but when the elderly priest finally realized what was happening, he instructed Samuel to respond to the Lord in humble obedience. (See 1 Samuel 3 for the full story.)

God also appeared to Abraham and Jacob in visions. In Genesis 15, the Lord communicated with the patriarch in a vision, saying, "Do not be afraid, Abram. I am your shield, your very great reward" (verse 1). Then God made a covenant with him, promising to bless Abraham's descendants and given them the Land of Canaan. Many years later, God appeared to Jacob in a vision at night in the desert of Beersheba. Reminiscent of the words He had spoken to Jacob's ancestor, God told Jacob not to fear and then promised to make him into a great nation (Genesis 46:1-4).

One of the most familiar examples of a vision in the New Testament is Peter's trance on a rooftop in the seaside village of Joppa, where he saw a sheet coming down from heaven, filled with all kinds of unclean animals that God had commanded His people not to eat. And yet in Peter's dream, a voice commanded Peter to "kill and eat."

Appalled, Peter said, "Surely not, Lord! I have never eaten anything impure or unclean."

But the Lord replied, "Do not call anything impure that God has made clean."

When the sheet was taken back up to heaven, Peter wondered what the vision meant—until the servants of a Gentile centurion named Cornelius arrived to speak to him. At that moment, Peter realized that God was telling him the Gentiles were no longer unclean in His eyes but that Christ had died to save all people, not just the Jews (Acts 10:9-28).

Many believers in the West are skeptical about visions, and that may be one reason why the Holy Spirit rarely uses this method to communicate with us in the twenty-first century. But throughout the Islamic world, where people are isolated from the gospel, God is reaching Muslims through dreams and visions, which are widely accepted as supernatural visitations from God.

Over the past decade, reports have indicated that unprecedented numbers of Muslims from the Middle East, North Africa, and Southeast Asia have been coming to faith in Christ through visions and dreams.[1] Muslims have a deep belief in the spiritual realm, so it makes sense that God would use these powerful and life-changing mediums to communicate His message to them. He knows exactly how to reach people like Amir and Hadassah with His truth and love!

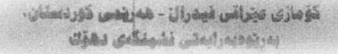

Arabic Bible

CHAPTER FOUR

A Shiite Warrior Renounces Jihad

Nasiriyah, Iraq

The clarion call to prayer resonated from a mosque minaret, piercing the predawn silence in the tranquil Iraqi desert. It was Friday, the holy day of prayer in the Islamic world. Sounds of shuffling feet echoed in the narrow alleyways and cobblestone streets of Nasiriyah, one of Iraq's holiest cities and home to the radical Shia sect of the Islamic faith.

Donning a white robe, leather sandals, and head covering, Sayeed stepped out into the tiny courtyard of his family's modest home. The first rays of golden sunlight illuminated the eastern horizon, chasing away the chill of night. Sayeed gazed upward and greeted the morning with a traditional Islamic prayer, thanking Allah for the breath in his body.

As he slowly opened the metal gate leading to the street, his heart began to pound. Today would be special. He and his friends planned to meet at the mosque for morning prayers and an inspirational message from the Koran. Word had spread around the city about that morning's speaker: Muqtada al-Sadr, a radical firebrand preacher and spiritual leader from Najaf.

The dusty streets swelled with faithful worshipers hurrying to the mosque. Old men sat in open doorways sipping hot tea and twirling prayer beads in their hands. The aroma of jasmine mixed with sweet-apple charcoal from hookah pipes hung in the morning air like mist. Women shooed curious children away from the mud-brick ovens where they were baking *nan* (flatbread)—God's food for the masses. Nasiriyah was awake and pulsating with life.

At the mosque, the burgeoning crowd poured through narrow stone arches leading into the ornate prayer room of the magnificent shrine. Before entering, everyone removed their shoes at the door, both in reverence to Allah and to avoid soiling the exquisite handwoven rugs that lined the floor. The ancient silk carpets, masterpieces of the fifth and sixth centuries, spoke of the glory of Islam and the people who lived in those days.

The muffled drone of conversation quickly erupted into shouts of *"Allahu akbar! Allahu akbar!"* ("God is great!") as Muqtada al-Sadr entered the mosque. The mystical aura of this fiery Lebanese cleric immediately captivated his followers, whipping them into a euphoric frenzy. Al-Sadr surveyed the crowd, his dark eyes flashing. The moment he began to speak, a hush fell over the room. His voice conveyed such passion and conviction that it seemed to consume worshipers with supernatural fire.

Sayeed listened in rapt attention as the infamous cleric challenged the true followers of Islam to resist the Americans, who had invaded Iraq for their own personal interests. With increasing intensity, he shouted for them to take up weapons and drive the infidels out of Iraq. At the climax of his impassioned message, his eyes swept around the room as he charged every worshiper to be a good Muslim, to sacrifice and devote himself to Allah and His prophet Muhammad, and if called upon, to become a martyr for Allah by joining the Mahdi Army and waging jihad in the streets of Najaf.

The message resonated in Sayeed's heart. He had never heard words like these before. Enraptured, the crowd once again began chanting, *"Allahu akbar! Allahu akbar!"* Sayeed joined in, his soul aflame with a spiritual fervor unlike anything he'd ever experienced. He felt so alive!

When al-Sadr finished speaking, worshipers rose to their feet and poured out of the mosque into the narrow streets of Nasiriyah. Resembling the running of the bulls in Spain, crazed young men, boiling with religious zeal and nationalistic pride, raced through the city, pumping their fists in the air and shouting. In blind devotion to al-Sadr's call for jihad, worshipers exchanged their white prayer robes and caps for black headscarves and grenade launchers.

On a street corner just minutes away from the mosque, recruiters for the Mahdi Army manned a table where young men could sign up on the spot. Sayeed felt a tug on his heart, sensing a new and greater calling for his life: to fight against the American infidels as a warrior for Allah.

Without a second thought, he walked over to the recruiting table and signed up to join the Mahdi Army. Wearing a traditional black headdress and holding a machine gun in one hand and a sword in the other, he had his photograph taken in front of a black backdrop decorated with Koranic verses. That morning, Sayeed wholeheartedly devoted his life to waging jihad as a Shiite warrior and even becoming a martyr, if it was the will of Allah.

For six years, Sayeed had studied in a *madrasah* (Islamic school), memorizing the Koran and preparing to become a priest (imam) in the local mosque in Nasiriyah. Now, at the age of twenty-two, he found himself in Najaf, carrying a Kalashnikov automatic rifle and fighting the jihad he had heard about but never dreamed he would be involved in.

Sayeed felt empowered by jihad. He was living out his faith through the barrel of a gun, fighting the imperialist Americans who had come to Najaf to capture Muqtada al-Sadr and conquer Sayeed's homeland. For the first time in his life as a Muslim, Sayeed's faith was real to him.

For several days, the fighting raged from street to street, alley to alley. Sayeed and his friends took up positions near the Imam Ali Shrine in Najaf, one of the holiest shrines in the Shia faith. They knew the Americans would never be allowed to attack this holy place, so they decided it would be safe to take refuge there.

But they had underestimated the American warriors. By early April, the shrine was surrounded by infidels, and a siege was imminent. More than 2,500 U.S. combat troops were encamped on the outskirts of Najaf, with thousands more standing ready to invade the city.[1]

The blistering-hot days melted into months, and before long, the siege began to take a toll on the Mahdi Army. By August, Sayeed and his fellow Shiite warriors were weary and demoralized. Staring into the darkness one night, Sayeed considered the Milky Way and the brilliant white crescent moon hanging against the backdrop of the pitch-black Iraqi sky. The universe looked so peaceful and celestial. Sayeed found himself wondering how Allah, the Creator of such beauty, could ordain violence and hatred as the way He chose to reveal Himself to humankind. Who was this God he was fighting for so passionately—and was so willing to die for?

At that moment, Sayeed became keenly aware of his mortality. The reckless courage he had felt just days before had evaporated, replaced by sober reality. He knew he would soon die if he continued fighting. Where would he spend eternity? The Koran said that if he died a martyr, he would go to paradise. But he wasn't so sure. His thoughts tormented him as he lay awake night after night, staring into the darkness and listening to the gunfire echoing in the distance.

One day, a friend in the army asked, "Sayeed, why is Islam so violent? Why do we discriminate against the women in our families?"

His friend's honest inquiry deepened Sayeed's frustration. He began to question the teaching he had received in the *madrasah*. He needed answers. Sayeed remembered an old religious man named Rushdi, whom his family had known for years. Rushdi had a very large library of ancient holy books; maybe he could help resolve Sayeed's doubts.

Slipping away from his post at the shrine one afternoon, Sayeed went to visit the old man. Rushdi spent most of his days in reflective solitude at home, and Sayeed found him sitting cross-legged on an antiquated carpet, frayed and threadbare from years of wear. Shafts of dusty sunlight seeped through the windows in the ceiling of the living room, silhouetting Rushdi's wrinkled, leathery face. Pushing aside the fabric covering that was draped across the entrance of the home, Sayeed greeted the elder.

"*As-salaam aleikum*, Rushdi." Sayeed bowed in respect. "May I come in?"

"*Wa aleikum as-salaam*," Rushdi replied with a twinkle in his eye. "Please come in and sit down, Sayeed. What brings you to see this old man?"

"I have questions about my faith and the teachings of the Koran," Sayeed told the sage.

Straining to rise, Rushdi feebly pushed himself to his feet. He shuffled across the carpet, pulling a small wooden stool over to a shelf piled high with papers and books. Reaching out a gnarled hand, he pulled an old leather-bound Arabic Bible from his archives.

"I was given this book by a man in Baghdad many, many years ago," Rushdi said, wiping a thick layer of dust off the cover. "I have found it to be a rose. The Koran is a sword. If you read this, I believe you will find the answers you are looking for. When you do, come back and tell me what you found."

Sayeed had never seen a Bible before. He took it in his hands and gently touched the smooth, dark leather. The book felt heavy, like gold—a priceless treasure. His eyes widened. A strange feeling came over him, but he couldn't identify it. Standing to leave, Sayeed looked straight into Rushdi's eyes. He sensed that he had met God that day.

Sayeed thanked the old man and left the house, making his

way back toward the shrine. He wanted to begin reading the Bible Rushdi gave him, but he knew this wasn't possible if he returned to his post. Glancing around to make sure no one was watching, he slipped down a side street and through a maze of alleyways until he reached his sleeping quarters. He sat down on his bed, gingerly opened the leather-bound volume, and immersed himself in the words on the yellowed pages.

The more he read, the more he wanted to read. His soul burned within him, and the hatred and fear that had consumed him for so many years began to melt away. His violent spirit found rest, and a strange new love for people flooded his heart. Sayeed didn't fully understand what had happened to him, but of one thing he was certain: The God he had so desperately searched for in Islam, he found in the Bible.

After a restless night of tossing and turning, Sayeed rose from his bed and wiped the sleep from his eyes as the morning call to prayer rang out from the Imam Ali Mosque. He felt a compelling desire to pray, but something was different this time. The day before, Sayeed had read the words of Issa (Jesus) in the Bible. Issa had said that Allah was near to Him and that anyone who sought Him could know Him personally. Sayeed could speak honestly to Allah, and Allah would hear him. For the first time in his life, Sayeed realized that prayer was real, not just an obligation he had to fulfill as a good Muslim.

As the *muezzin's* call echoed in the early morning air, Sayeed bowed his head and spoke to God in a simple way, as if he were speaking to a friend. A sense of peace washed over Sayeed as he lifted his concerns and requests to God, thanking Allah for revealing

Himself in His Word.

After Sayeed finished his prayers, he realized that he couldn't return to his post with the Mahdi Army. He knew he would be regarded as a deserter and that soldiers would hunt him down and shoot him as a traitor to Allah. Fearing for his life, Sayeed fled to a distant relative's house for refuge.

Several weeks later, Sayeed returned to Rushdi's home and told him about the incredible things he had learned in the Bible. Rushdi raised his hand and then leaned over and scribbled on a crumpled piece of paper.

Pulling Sayeed close, Rushdi whispered in his ear, "There is a group of people in Baghdad you need to meet. This address will get you close. Look for a white cross and then listen for singing; there you will find them. Now, go in peace."

As Sayeed turned to leave, he and Rushdi made eye contact. Rushdi smiled and then closed his eyes.

Before dawn the next morning, Sayeed made his way to the bus station, where he bought a ticket to the sprawling metropolis of Baghdad. Crammed beyond capacity, the bus couldn't hold one more person or thing. Everyone seemed to be on a pilgrimage that day—men, women, and children. Even goats, some chickens—and a car engine.

As he waited to board the bus, Sayeed reached into his pocket and pulled out the crumpled paper Rushdi had given him the day before. Who were these people in Baghdad? Had they also found God in the Bible? Filled with hope, Sayeed sensed that a new chapter in his life was about to unfold.

The bus was scheduled to depart at first light, as soon as the nightly travel curfew was lifted and the roads had reopened. Rogue checkpoints on the highways would be safer and easier to pass through during the daytime. Sensible Iraqis did not travel at night. That was when the Devil's sons came out to play—suicide bombers, snipers, kidnappers. They all exacted a deadly toll. Leaving early also made the excruciating heat of the Iraqi desert more bearable. Temperatures that day would likely reach 119 degrees Fahrenheit.

As soon as Sayeed boarded the bus, he collapsed onto a tattered seat near the back and leaned his head against a dirty window. Sleepless nights and the stresses of war had left him exhausted. As the bus made its way out of Najaf, the stifling diesel fumes and searing heat mingled into a hypnotic potion, and soon Sayeed was fast asleep.

It seemed that he had just drifted off when he was jolted awake by the harsh voice of a soldier demanding his papers. The bus had stopped at a rogue military checkpoint, and soldiers wearing black hoods were interrogating all the passengers. Sayeed reluctantly handed over his documents, knowing he could be shot if the soldier discovered that he was an army deserter. But after examining the papers and asking a few questions, the soldier moved on to the next passenger. Sayeed breathed a silent prayer of thanks to God.

After more than an hour of interrogation, the soldiers finally allowed the bus to continue on its way. In a belch of black exhaust, the ancient vehicle lumbered onto the bomb-cratered highway, heading toward Baghdad. Sayeed tried to sleep, but he was too wound up. Instead he passed the time thinking about the strangers he was traveling so far to meet.

Listen for singing, Rushdi had told him. What kind of people sang in the middle of a war? He doubted that such a group of people existed, and yet he had to find out. Rushdi had seemed so certain!

It was late afternoon when the bus approached the outskirts of Baghdad. A trip that should have taken only a couple of hours ended up taking all day because of the bad road conditions and repeated stops at military checkpoints.

As they approached the city, Sayeed was stunned by its vastness. Sprawling out like huge anthill, Baghdad swallowed the desert. Love it or hate it, millions of people called Baghdad home. It was amazing to think that Nasiriyah's tiny population could fit into one of Baghdad's smaller suburbs.

Still in the throes of al-Qaida uprisings against the new Iraqi government, Baghdad was a dangerous place. With its traffic-clogged streets and stifling pollution, it seemed like another planet to Sayeed. He felt intimidated in such a large city, but he was determined to find the people Rushdi had told him about. Would they truly know the God of the Bible?

Suddenly, a violent jolt rocked the bus just outside Baghdad. Veering wildly to the side of the road, the bus skidded into a ditch in a choking cloud of dust. Less than fifty yards away, huge billows of thick black smoke spiraled upward, blotting out the afternoon sun. Gunfire erupted in every direction. Bloodied people screamed and scattered. Men carried small children with severed limbs; women threw their arms into the air and wailed for their dead husbands. One old lady sat motionless in the middle of the road, stunned from the shock.

An improvised explosive device (IED) had found its mark: an American military convoy of fuel trucks near a busy food market just ahead. Within minutes, American military vehicles and Iraqi police rushed past the bus to the chaotic scene.

Sayeed began to weep. He had seen all of this before, too many times. Radical Muslims and terrorists, death and destruction, brother against brother, innocent people killed. But now he was a changed man on a different journey.

The horrific scene still replaying in his mind, Sayeed collected himself and found another bus for the final leg of his trip. He once again took out the wrinkled paper Rushdi had given him and studied it carefully.

The bus maneuvered through the congested streets of Baghdad, finally arriving at Sayeed's destination: Sadr City. Stepping down from the bus, Sayeed glanced around. *Look for a white cross and then listen for singing*, Rushdi had told him. Sayeed didn't see a cross or hear any singing. His heart sank as a dark cloud of discouragement enveloped him.

Suddenly, something or someone spoke to him, directing him to small tea stand across the street. As Sayeed approached the vendor to order a cup of tea, the man smiled and said, "You will find what you are looking for soon. Just follow this street to its end, and as you come to the corner, stop and listen. Then you will hear it."

Sayeed gazed in the direction the man indicated and then turned to thank him for his instructions. But the tea vendor had vanished. Could he have been an angel?

Shaken, Sayeed stumbled down the street. His heart was pounding just as it had the day he and his friends had gone to the mosque in Nasiriyah to hear Muqtada al-Sadr speak. But this time was different. Sayeed knew that the God he was searching for would be in this place. He quickened his pace to a jog and then a full-out run. He could barely contain his excitement.

When Sayeed reached the end of the street, he looked around frantically. And then he spotted it. Just a short distance down the street, near the corner, a small building with a white cross on top came into view. Illuminated by a spotlight, the building was silhouetted against the scarlet reds and violets of twilight in the western sky. Sayeed had never seen anything so beautiful in his life. Rushdi had been right! The people who knew the God of the Bible were here!

Sayeed's heart was pounding so hard, he thought it would explode through his chest. Breathing deeply to calm himself, Sayeed listened intently…and waited. Then he heard it: people singing, just as Rushdi had told him! The songs were unlike any he had ever heard—songs of joy and praise to Allah, songs of life and hope.

Drawing closer to the building, Sayeed felt a warm sensation spreading through his body, like the heat of a campfire on a cold night in the desert. Walking cautiously up the cement steps, Sayeed reached for the latch and slowly opened the door. The people inside turned to see who had entered.

Even though he was a stranger, they greeted him warmly and made him feel as if he was one of their own. Sayeed sensed that he was home. He had finally found what he had been searching for all of his life—a place of peace and safety, a community of love, and most of all, the true God.

The years he had spent in the radical Islamic *madrasahs* learning about Allah suddenly faded away. His new friends spoke about the God who loved him and sent His Son, Issa, to save him. Allah became real to Sayeed that night as these believers taught him what it meant to become a student of the Bible and a disciple of Issa.

When Sayeed returned to Nasiriyah, he knew he couldn't tell his family about his decision to follow Jesus. If his family and friends, or the Shia clerics, discovered that he had converted to Christianity, his life would be in danger. He continued to read his Bible and learn more of God in secret, but he lived in constant fear of discovery and death.

Several months later, Sayeed decided that he had to leave Nasiriyah. Although he felt closer to God and knew his life had changed, the daily loneliness and desire to be with his friends at the church in Baghdad became unbearable.

Sayeed told his family that he was moving to Baghdad, disguising the reason for his decision just as he had disguised the reason for his frequent visits to the city whenever his parents had asked. It wasn't easy to hide the truth from them, especially when they kept bombarding him with questions. But he couldn't risk their finding out the real reason.

As soon as Sayeed moved to Baghdad, he joined the tiny fellowship of believers near Sadr City and became one of the young church leaders. Not long after this, he met a beautiful young lady named Hava, who radiated the same joy he had found. As he conversed with her, he discovered that she and her family were Sunni Muslims who had become believers the previous year through supernatural dreams and visions of Jesus.

Hava's story amazed Sayeed, and the more he learned about her, the more convinced he was that God had brought them together. Sayeed and Hava soon fell in love, and in 2007, with the blessings of her father and family, they married. They continue to worship with other believers at the fellowship in Sadr City and are growing daily in their faith.

Once a Shiite warrior in Muqtada al-Sadr's Mahdi Army, Sayeed is now a faithful servant of Jesus Christ. Despite the constant dangers and death threats that he and his wife face from the Shia community, they rejoice to be counted worthy to serve the Lord. Sayeed and Hava are both committed to returning to Nasiriyah to open an outreach center, where they hope to share God's love among their people.

As Sayeed so humbly put it, "I once was willing to be a martyr for Islam and my radical Shia beliefs; now I am ready to be a martyr for Jesus, who died for me."

Throughout Iraq, God is calling people like Sayeed to walk in the footsteps of their ancestor Abraham, who left behind his homeland, his relatives, and his religious and cultural heritage, entrusting himself and his future to the living God. Like Abraham, they have no idea where God is leading them, but in faith they are following Jesus, no matter the cost.

In that same spirit of faith, Sayeed responded to God's call, leaving behind his own religious heritage to embrace a radically different life as a follower of Christ. Laying down the sword of jihad, Sayeed finally found what he had been searching for all his life: a relationship with the true God.

Sayeed's home of Nasiriyah and the holy city of Najaf are located in a region of modern-day Iraq historically referred to as the Land of Elam. According to Genesis 10, Elam was the first of five sons born to Noah's son Shem. The great flood had wiped the earth clean of every living person and thing, except for Noah, his wife, their three sons—Shem, Ham, and Japheth—and their sons' wives.

After the flood, God commanded the descendants of Noah to repopulate the earth. Ham's descendants settled in the region of modern-day Africa; Japheth's descendants spread throughout modern-day Turkey and western Asia; and Shem's descendants—the Semites, from whom the Jewish and Arab people came—settled in the region just to the north of the Persian Gulf.

As I mentioned earlier, in ancient times, the Sumerian civilization, known for its advanced technology and social systems, populated this region. The Sumerians were credited with a number of innovations, including the cuneiform writing system, the plow, the wheel, and agricultural irrigation canals.

Today, this Venice of the Middle East, as it is sometimes called because of its system of canals, is home to more than one million people, many of whom live in Iraq's third largest city, Basra. The people of this region are predominantly of Arab descent, belonging to the Adnanite or Qahtanite tribes. Economically, Basra has many oil wells, as well as a vast number of untapped petroleum reserves. According to some estimates, up to 80 percent of the fields in this area remain unexplored. The top agricultural products in this fertile region include rice, corn, millet, barley, and dates.

As we discovered in the introduction, another important city in the land of Elam was Ur of the Chaldeans—home of the patriarch Abraham. Apart from biblical references, little was known about this ancient city until shortly after World War I, when a team of British and American archaeologists, led by Sir Charles Leonard Woolley, discovered a massive mound of bricks and rubble about 230 miles south of Baghdad.

Further exploration revealed the ancient city of Ur, including nearly two thousand burial sites, sixteen of which were royal tombs.

Looking at the ruins of ancient Ur, it's hard to imagine that it was once a bustling metropolitan city surrounded by lush tropical gardens and lined with fig trees and date palms, irrigated by a system of canals that drew water from a nearby river. Temples, storage houses, schools, and markets were abundant. Sprawling villas with open roofs stretched endlessly throughout the city. Ziggurats—pyramid-like structures predating those in Egypt—provided those in Ur with an elevated view of the universe.

When God called Abraham to leave Ur and journey to a far-off land—the land of Shem—He promised to bless all nations of the earth through this man of faith. Judaism, Christianity, and Islam—the world's monotheistic religions—trace their roots back to him, and from his line of descendants would come the Savior of the world. Not only is Abraham the father of Isaac's and Ishmael's descendants; "he is the father of all who believe" (Romans 4:11).

As an Iraqi, Sayeed is a natural-born descendant of Abraham, but as a Christian, he has also become a spiritual descendant of this man whose faith was counted as righteousness before God (Romans 4:18-24). Sayeed's transformation from a warrior of Allah to a servant of Christ is nothing short of miraculous, and yet all over the Middle East, God is calling young men and women to lay down their weapons of jihad and follow Him.

Friday prayers –Tehran

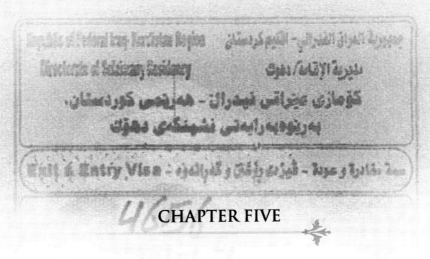

CHAPTER FIVE

A New Identity

Baghdad, Iraq

Saddam Hussein had just been hanged, but Iraq was a ticking time bomb. In spite of taking small parts of Baghdad from insurgents, the Americans and their coalition forces had to retreat to the Green Zone on the west side of the city. The eastern half of Baghdad, including Sadr City, was spiraling into chaos. The Sunni uprising in Fallujah had proven to be more of a fight than anyone wanted, including the Americans. Muqtada al-Sadr's radical Shiite Mahdi Army ruled the streets and holy shrines of Najaf. The al-Anbar Province, overrun with al-Qaida fighters, smoldered like a hot bed of coals. Basra, in the south of the country, wasn't safe either.

It would take months—or years—for the small military gains of coalition forces to be felt throughout Baghdad. Islamic insurgents had taken advantage of the city's congested streets and honeycomb alleyways, creating sophisticated networks to continue their campaign of terror and resistance. Iraq was free from Saddam Hussein—but not from tyranny.

Another Hussein lived in the midst of the chaos. Like many Iraqis, his identification card classified him as a Sunni Muslim by birth. Although Hussein was considered a minority in Iraq, he enjoyed a relatively good life with his parents and siblings. Their home on the west side of Baghdad was located just across the Tigris River in a predominantly Sunni neighborhood. A few Assyrian Orthodox Christians and Shiite Muslims lived among them, but they were decent people and usually kept to themselves.

Hussein's neighbors never practiced their faith openly, but Hussein knew that the Christians celebrated Christmas and Easter, and the Shias commemorated the Day of Ashura, when the prophet Muhammad's grandson was martyred. The Christians had spoken to Hussein from time to time about knowing God personally, and this had piqued Hussein's interest. But he was a Sunni Muslim, and in the midst of war, survival was all that mattered—not religion. Everyone was living in a state of fear about what might happen in the future.

Before the American invasion, people had traveled safely around the sprawling city of Baghdad. Traffic jams had been the biggest problem. But after the invasion, only military vehicles and convoys had the freedom to canvas the city. For civilians, traveling by car, bus, or taxi became a luxury. It could take hours just to walk to the corner market for bread; that is, if one survived the suicide bombers. Steel-reinforced concrete barriers and massive concrete walls erected around the city became virtual stoplights, denying average Iraqis access to many sections of Baghdad.

American military checkpoints ignited outrage among some Iraqis, who felt harassed and humiliated by the invasive searches and questioning. In this part of the world, it was unacceptable for a man to speak to a woman unless he was her husband or a close relative. Any American soldier who questioned an Iraqi woman showed flagrant disregard for deeply held cultural and religious norms. Such violations were not easily forgiven.

On the darker side, former members of the Iraqi military had organized their own renegade militias, taking advantage of the lawlessness and turmoil that ruled in many parts of Iraq. With the American military hunkered down in the Green Zone, the rest of Baghdad—and Iraq—was ripe for the taking. War was a lucrative business for criminals looking to steal artifacts from local museums and tap into billions of dollars in oil revenues. Unable to fight back, innocent Iraqis could only watch in helpless despair as their nation was pillaged and destroyed.

Armed militias soon took over Hussein's neighborhood. At first they demanded small bribes in return for the privilege of traveling around the city. Those who were willing and able to pay the money created problems for those who either didn't have the money or refused to pay. Tempers flared as the militias grew bolder and more violent. Many of the insurgents began wearing black hoods to conceal their identities.

Then what Hussein and his neighbors had been dreading finally happened. Rumors spread throughout the community about a Shiite man who had argued with one of the militia members over a bribe. The man had been missing for several days before his body, along with the bodies of his wife and three children, was found in an abandoned field. All of them had been shot through the head, execution style. They had been murdered not for money but because they were Shiites.

Now, a different kind of war was being waged in Iraq—a war of revenge. The streets of Baghdad had become a theater for centuries-old tribal and religious scores to be settled. Sunni against Shia, Kurds against Arabs, Muslims against Christians, Catholics against evangelicals, family against family. An eye for an eye, a tooth for a tooth, hell had been unleashed in Baghdad.

With Saddam dead and gone, the Sunnis became instant targets of ethnic reprisals for the atrocities committed against other religious and ethnic groups during Saddam's brutal reign. Neighbors began to suspect one another of giving information to the authorities—whoever they were. No one knew.

One day, as Hussein was on his way to visit a friend on the other side of Baghdad, he came upon a line of people being funneled into a narrow series of concrete barriers. It was a new mobile checkpoint that had been set up in his neighborhood overnight. Although the guards were dressed in official Iraqi military clothing, Hussein sensed that something was terribly wrong. Shia militias often used Iraqi uniforms and equipment to disguise their true identity.

After Hussein had taken his place in line, he noticed that all the men were being segregated into two groups and told to sit in a field nearby.

"What is happening?" Hussein asked an elderly man in front of him.

"They are checking ID cards to see whether we are Sunni or Shia," the man replied.

Hussein wondered why Iraqis would do such a thing to their own people, and then his thoughts darkened. Maybe the militias were going to rob them, kidnap them, or relocate them to another part of Baghdad. Or maybe something much worse! He shuddered to entertain such thoughts, but this was Baghdad. Anything was possible.

Fear gripped Hussein's heart. He didn't know what to do. No one knew what to do. But as he approached the checkpoint, he suddenly realized there was only one thing he could do.

The Shia guard took his ID card, glanced at it, and then shouted, "You are Sunni?"

"No, I am a Christian!" Hussein replied, trying to sound convincing.

The guard stared at Hussein with a puzzled look on his face and then broke into laughter.

"How you can be Christian?" he scoffed. "You are Muslim. You are Sunni."

"No, I am Christian!" Hussein insisted. "I have accepted Jesus; I am no longer Muslim!"

Hussein knew his claim was absurd, and during Saddam's regime, it would have sealed his fate. But today he hoped it would save his life. Recalling what his Assyrian Christian neighbors had told him about Jesus, Hussein sensed that God was at his side helping him.

"What did you do to convert?" the guard asked in a curious tone of voice.

At first the question took Hussein by surprise, but when he looked at the guard, he realized that the man was genuinely interested.

"I know about God from the Koran," Hussein replied, "but I never thought I could know Him personally. One day, my Assyrian Christian neighbors told me that to know God I only had to believe in His Son, Jesus, and if I did, I would be saved. Today I believe this is true!"

"My friend," said the guard, "today you have been saved by this name. You may go." He handed back the papers and waved Hussein through the checkpoint.

As Hussein walked away from the checkpoint a free man, he breathed a prayer of thanks to God and vowed that he would learn more about this Jesus, who had saved him and given him a new identity.

Years later, Hussein still vividly remembers how God miraculously spared him from certain death. He heard rumors that many of the men rounded up at the checkpoint that day in Baghdad had vanished, and he suspected that they had been executed. All of them had been Sunni Muslims.

At the time, Hussein didn't know why his life had been spared, but he longed to know more about the Christian faith and this Jesus he had confessed as his Savior. Soon he found a group of Christians to meet with and shared his story with them.

Like the thief hanging on the cross next to Jesus, Hussein's life hung in eternity's scales. He was condemned to die because he was a Sunni Muslim. In desperation, he called out the only words he could think of to save him—"I am a Christian!"—and God spared his life. That name led Hussein to Jesus, a community of believers, and a brand-new life and identity!

Issue Date : 30/9/07

Hussein's story is not only a powerful illustration of God's miraculous protection and deliverance, but it also reveals the creative ways He draws people to Himself. Out of desperation, Hussein claimed to be a Christian to keep from being killed as a Sunni Muslim. But God had a much bigger purpose in mind for Hussein that day at the military checkpoint. He wanted to give this young Muslim a brand-new identity in Christ that would deliver him from spiritual death—an eternity separated from God—and fill him with such incredible hope and joy that his life would never be the same.

In the early days of the Iraq War, many Iraqis like Hussein rejoiced that the U.S. military and their coalition partners had broken the steel grip of Saddam Hussein's brutal regime. After decades of oppression under Saddam, many Iraqis began to feel the winds of hope and freedom blowing across the land. But when the dust cleared and the country began to emerge from the fog of war, they began to realize that the U.S. presence would not guarantee the stability they had been hoping for. Unrest and violence continued to terrorize the people of Iraq—Sunni, Shia, and Kurds alike. Even today, peace in many parts of Iraq hangs by a fragile thread. Ethnic reprisals, suicide bombings, political infighting, and unfulfilled promises of Iraqi officials and Western governments continually threaten to derail the hard-fought progress the Iraqi people have made over the past eight years. Mistrust and disillusionment eat away at the hope many felt when Saddam was defeated.

As Hussein discovered, being a Sunni Muslim in post-war Iraq can be dangerous…even lethal. After decades of Sunni brutality against the Shia and Kurdish populations of Iraq, a violent backlash was unleashed soon after Saddam and his regime were toppled. Being identified as a Sunni on the streets of Baghdad since then has resulted in mistreatment and death for untold numbers of people. Shiite militias have had no qualms about evening up the score.

In such an atmosphere, it's no wonder that Hussein did whatever he could to survive, even if it meant embracing an identity he never would have considered claiming as his own in another situation. At that checkpoint, God brought Hussein into a freedom that surpassed his ethnic and religious heritage and opened up an entirely different way of seeing the world.

As the apostle Paul wrote in Galatians 3:28, "[In Christ], there is neither Jew nor Greek, [nor Sunni, Shia, or Kurd], slave nor free, male nor female, for you are all one in Jesus Christ."

Like Hussein, hundreds of Muslims in Iraq and around the world are discovering a new life and identity in Christ. They are realizing that Jesus has broken down the religious and ethnic barriers that humans build and has made a way for Sunnis, Shias, and Kurds to live in peace.

For the first time in their lives, many Iraqis, who have wandered in the darkness of Islam their entire lives, are experiencing freedom to worship the God they have been longing to know. But many are still searching in the darkness for true freedom and an identity that rises above the labels of Sunni, Shia, or Kurd.

Real liberation for the Iraqi people will never be achieved through America's political and military assistance, or even by defeating al-Qaida and other Islamic extremists. It can only be found in the name of Jesus! As Hussein discovered that day at the checkpoint, nothing is impossible for God! He can even use a case of assumed identity to accomplish His purposes for those He loves.

Mosque

CHAPTER SIX

Priest of the Mosque

Mosul, Iraq

Afternoon sunlight filtered through decorative wrought-iron windows, dappling the ornate rugs that lined the floor of the mosque. Abdul folded his hands over his chest and then bowed, touching his forehead to the ground as he recited words from the Koran. The Islamic ritual was second nature to him.

As the worshipers around him intoned prayers to Allah, Abdul silently breathed a prayer to Issa (Jesus): *Thank you for being the God I can know. I am so grateful that You are the God who hears me.*

When Friday prayers ended, Abdul rose to his feet, folded his prayer rug, and headed toward the exit, passing under beautiful mosaic arches and slowly descending the steps of the ancient Islamic mosque. His conversation with God had given him hope for another day.

Raised in an extremely strict Muslim home near Mosul, Iraq, Abdul had always been a good Muslim. From the time he was a small boy, his father wanted him to become an imam (priest) at the local mosque. At the age of sixteen, Abdul joined the Muslim Brotherhood and enrolled in an Islamic university to further his understanding of the Koran. After years of intensive study, he finally achieved his father's dream: He was elevated to the prestigious position of imam in his hometown mosque.

Every Friday, Abdul read from the Koran and expounded upon the virtues of Islam to those who had come to pray, and yet he found little fulfillment in his role as imam. He was serving Allah and observing all the requirements of the Islamic faith, but he felt empty. The first whispers of doubt entered his heart, but he didn't know where to turn for answers.

Then one summer afternoon, everything changed when Abdul went to the city market to buy fresh vegetables. As he walked among the vendors, he noticed a man who stood out from the crowd. No one seemed to give the man a second glance. But to Abdul, well versed in the Koran's teachings about spirits and angelic beings, this stranger seemed more like a jinn than a mere man. His face glowed with an inner light, and his eyes reflected the sun. Raven black hair contrasted with clothing of the purest white. Even though Abdul knew that a true jinn could be good or evil, he was drawn to the brightly shining stranger like a moth to a flame.

Not without a little fear, Abdul dared to address him. "What is your name, sir?" he asked in a humble tone.

"I am Hani, from Cairo," the man replied.

"What are you—an Egyptian—doing in northern Iraq?" Abdul asked.

Hani answered with gentle confidence, "I am a messenger of God, sent to tell others about His love and mercy. Do you know this God of whom I speak?"

Hani's straightforward response took Abdul by surprise, but the simple question forced him to think. After a moment's hesitation, he answered, "I teach in the local mosque, I pray five times every day, and I give alms to the poor. I fast during Ramadan, and five years ago, I made my first hajj to Mecca. I try to be a good Muslim; I believe I know God."

"You have told me all the things you do for God," Hani replied, "but you have not told me who God is. I perceive that you do not know Him... But you can. If you wish to know God, you must ask to know Him."

Abdul was stunned. Hani's words answered a question that had troubled Abdul for many years. How can a human being truly know the God of the universe? From studying the Koran and other Islamic writings, Abdul had learned everything that was required to be a good Muslim. And yet he never felt that his obedience had brought him any closer to God. Allah was distant and unknowable, a mysterious being who was impossible to reach. Abdul realized that he did not know his god, and yet he was this god's slave.

As Abdul pondered Hani's words, the stranger turned and simply walked away. Abdul ran after him, wanting to ask more questions, but just as mysteriously as this messenger had appeared, he vanished into the crowd. Abdul was left standing in the middle of the marketplace. People scurried around him, too busy with their shopping to take any notice of him. When he finally turned toward home, the words of the stranger were still ringing in his ears. *You can know God!* Could it be true?

Abdul told no one of his encounter with the messenger from Cairo, not even his wife. He returned to his normal routine of teaching in the mosque and leading Friday prayers. But he couldn't forget his conversation with the mysterious Hani. Abdul recalled Hani's words: *If you want to know God, you must ask to know Him.* Abdul yearned for such an experience.

Summer gave way to the cooler days of autumn, and on an evening in late October, Abdul had his first real encounter with Hani's God. After completing afternoon prayers at the mosque, Abdul set out for a walk in the remote hills behind his home. Finding a small outcropping of rocks, he climbed up to watch the sun set over the western plains. Mingling shades of red and pink turned the sky to a royal purple, and in the midst of the stunning display, Abdul sensed the nearness of God.

For the first time in his life, Abdul called out, "God, I know many things about You, but I want to know who You are. Please, let me see You!"

As twilight plunged the landscape into shades of gray, Abdul stumbled down the rocky slopes to his home. Inside, his children were gathered around the television, watching a satellite station from Amman, Jordan. At this time of the evening, they usually watched cartoons, but the program had been preempted by a religious broadcast. On the screen, an elderly man wearing long clerical robes began to speak.

At first, Abdul thought the man was another Islamic teacher extolling the virtues of Islam, but moments later, Abdul was listening intently as Father Yasan described the differences between the Bible and the Koran in flowing Arabic. The man spoke of a God who loved the world so much that He sent His own Son to die for the sins of humanity. Those who believed in this Jesus would be given new life—salvation.

Father Yasan explained that all one had to do was ask for this gift of salvation, and God would freely give it. Abdul was amazed. *I just asked God to reveal Himself to me, and now this man is telling me that if I accept His Son, He will come into my life. This religion has no requirements; all I have to do is ask and believe!*

At the end of the program, Abdul learned that Father Yasan was a teacher from Egypt, and he wondered whether Hani and this teacher knew each other.

For an entire year, Abdul secretly watched Father Yasan's program, learning more about the Bible and its teachings. Just as Hani had said, it was possible to know God, but even more amazing, God wanted to know Abdul. Still, many of the things Abdul heard were strange and difficult for him to understand. Questions began to multiply in his mind: *The Bible says that God sent His Son to die for me, but how could God have a Son? God did not have a wife, and even if He did, why would He allow evil men to kill His only Son for sins He did not commit? How could Jesus love me so much? Why would He love me at all?*

One night, while in a deep sleep, Abdul had a vision. His body was stretched out, suspended on a white cross. A heavy sensation flowed over him, and he couldn't move his lifeless limbs. Abdul gazed helplessly at a figure standing at the foot of the cross. The man shone with the brightness of the noonday sun. Speaking to Abdul in a soft voice, he said, "Abdul, do not fear. You have asked God to show Himself to you, and I have come to do just that. I am the God you seek. I am Jesus, and I am here to take your place."

Jesus showed him the cuts and bruises that marred his back, and then He revealed the nail scars on His hands. With incredible gentleness, he picked up Abdul, carried him to safety, and then took his place on the cross.

Waking in a cold sweat, Abdul left his bed and paced the darkened room. Now he knew what it meant to know God. The Islamic religion had enslaved him all his life, but the true God wanted Abdul for himself, not for what Abdul could do for Him.

The next morning, Abdul began looking at the world in a whole new way. It was as if he had been living with scales over his eyes, but now they had been removed, and he could finally see. He regarded everything with new appreciation. The sun seemed to shine brighter, and colors were more vivid. Even his wife and children were more beautiful and dear to his heart. He felt closer to God, and yet he still felt incomplete. *There has to be more*, he thought.

What Abdul wanted now was to find someone else who believed—someone like Hani or Father Yasan. He had heard that there were Christians in northern Iraq, but he didn't know how to find them. He was at the center of the Muslim community, and all of his acquaintances were people who worshiped at the mosque.

Remembering how the Lord had heard his prayer when he asked

God to reveal Himself, Abdul offered a new prayer: "God, please let me meet someone in this city who is a follower of Jesus."

Later that day, Abdul brought his children to the library. They were reading a book on local folklore when Abdul overheard a discussion between two men at a neighboring table. Leaning toward the table to catch what was being said, Abdul couldn't believe his ears. The men were talking about Jesus! They weren't wearing robes like Father Yasan, and they didn't have shining faces like Hani, but their words were full of life. Once again, Abdul had asked, and God had answered.

As the men stood to leave, Abdul hurried to follow, eager to speak with them. He was half-afraid they would disappear as Hani had, but this time, when Abdul stretched out his hand, he touched one of the men's shoulders. The stranger from the library turned and looked curiously at him.

"Sir, I must have a word with you!" Abdul earnestly pleaded. "I heard you speaking of a man named Jesus. Could you please talk to me for a few moments? I have been trying to learn more about God my whole life, and I must know more about this Jesus you speak of. Will you tell me about Him?"

The man smiled and said, "I will gladly talk to you about God. My name is Daud, and I'm a pastor at a church in Assam. When can we meet?"

"Then you are a teacher like me?" Abdul exclaimed in wonder. "If so, you can explain all the things about the Bible I need to know, yes?"

"I will be happy to study the Bible with you and share everything I know," Pastor Daud assured him. "God has brought us together."

Once a week, Abdul and Pastor Daud met secretly in the nearby mountains to study God's Word together, and each time, God opened Abduls eyes to the truth of His Word and the reality of His Son. Abdul learned that God was more interested in having a relationship with him than in the empty religious rituals Abdul performed to please Him.

In time, Abdul's wife, Sadiyah, noticed subtle changes in her husband and began asking questions. Abdul knew that he would soon have to reveal his newfound faith in Jesus to her.

Late one afternoon, Abdul returned to the mountainside where he had his first real encounter with God the year before. In humility, Abdul cried out to God again, "God, You revealed Yourself to me here on this mountain. Now I am asking You to reveal Yourself to my wife and family. I don't know how You will do this, but please show Your love to them as You did with me."

When Abdul returned home that night, Sadiyah and the children met him at the door. He immediately noticed the inquisitive looks on their faces.

"Where have you been Abdul, and why is your face shining?" Sadiyah asked.

At that moment, Abdul realized that God was answering his prayer. Dropping to his knees, Abdul joyfully proclaimed his faith in the true God to his entire family.

Sadiyah fell into his arms and began to cry as she kissed her husband's cheeks. "I knew something had happened to you the day you watched that man from Egypt on the television. You have become a much better man since then, and that is why I want to know your God too!"

That day, Abdul's entire family invited God's Son into their lives and began to grow in God's grace and love.

Years after his encounters with Hani and Pastor Daub, Abdul is still an imam at the local mosque, teaching from the Koran and observing all of the traditions and requirements of Islam. But he and his family are also secret followers of Christ.

Abdul isn't afraid to die for his faith in Jesus, but he senses that it's not yet time for him to reveal his conversion to Christianity. Abdul wants to be able to introduce Jesus to other Muslims, and to do that, he must stay alive. He is living out his faith in one of the most unique ways imaginable: becoming "all things to all men" in order to save some (1 Corinthians 9:22).

Many worshipers at the mosque who respect Abdul have noticed a change in him, though they don't know what—or who—is behind this transformation. Abdul prays that someday Issa will reveal Himself to other Muslims in the same miraculous way He revealed Himself to Abdul.

Like Hani, Abdul has a message for those who are longing for more as they go through the motions of faith: You can know the living God! All you have to do is ask! And like Pastor Daud, Abdul stands ready to share the truth of God that can only be found in the Bible.

Abdul's people, the Kurds of northern Iraq, have endured great suffering throughout the centuries, particularly during Saddam

Hussein's reign of terror. His brutal treatment of these fiercely independent tribal Sunni Muslims has been well documented. During the 1980s alone, more than three hundred thousand Kurds perished in Saddam's forced labor camps, as well as from chemical warfare, genocide, and summary executions.

Most Americans have seen disturbing images of the chemical attacks that occurred in 1988 at Halabja, a town of approximately eighty thousand located near the Iranian border. During a three-day period, the town was attacked with conventional bombs, artillery shells, and chemical agents, including mustard gas, sarin, and VX. In September of 1988, Human Rights Watch and Time magazine reported that as many as seven thousand people died in these horrific attacks. Several thousand more would perish in the aftermath from illness and disease. By 2003, only fifty thousand Kurds remained in Halabja.

The Kurds, numbering close to 25 million, are considered the world's largest people group without a nation to call their own. In 1920, at the end of World War I, the Ottoman Empire and the Allied Forces signed a peace treaty—the Treaty of Sèvres—promising the Kurds an independent state following the creation of the modern nations of Syria, Iraq, and Kuwait. But nearly one hundred years later, the Kurdish people continue their struggle for a national homeland.

Kurdish territory is currently divided among the modern states of Turkey, Iraq, Iran, and Syria, as well as the southern republics of the former Soviet Union. Just over four million Kurds live in Iraq, constituting about 23 percent of the population. Since the first Gulf War in 1990 and the overthrow of Saddam Hussein in 2003, the

Kurds have enjoyed a relatively peaceful existence and have begun to flourish once again.

Although Abdul is living out his faith in secret, in a way, his story reminds me of the famous Old Testament story about Daniel. (To read the story in its entirety, see Daniel 6.) One of the Jewish exiles from Judah, Daniel had been taken captive by King Nebuchadnezzar and deported to Babylon in 605 BC. When the Babylonian Empire fell to the Persians in 539 BC, the Mede king Darius rose to power in Babylon. Respected throughout the land, Daniel served as one of three government administrators under King Darius. Daniel performed his responsibilities so exceptionally that the king planned to put him in charge of the entire kingdom. But jealous men plotted against Daniel and succeeded in persuading the king to sign a decree prohibiting everyone in the kingdom from praying to any god or human except the king. Anyone found disobeying this decree was to be thrown into a den of hungry lions.

In spite of the decree, Daniel continued to pray to his God three times a day in full view of everyone. The government officials spied on Daniel to catch him in the act and then went immediately to the king to report what they had seen. Even though Darius had great respect for Daniel, he was bound by the law of the Medes and Persians to uphold his decision, so he gave the order to throw Daniel into the lion's den.

After a sleepless night, Darius ran to the den at first light to find out what had happened to Daniel. To the king's amazement, the young man was alive. Daniel's God had intervened, saving Daniel from the jaws of death.

Daniel resumed his prominent role as administrator in the

kingdom of the Medes and Persians. As chief among the wise men and astrologers, his influence and leadership would be felt for centuries to come, culminating with the journey of the Wise Men from the east—the kingdom of the Persians—who followed a star to a little Judean town called Bethlehem and found the Messiah they had been searching for.

Whether in the courts of an ancient Persian king or in the pulpit of a modern Islamic mosque, God's people are often called to serve Him in the most unlikely places!

Kurdish Muslim - N. Iraq

CHAPTER SEVEN

Nadim's
Secret Faith

Najaf, Iraq

On a late September afternoon, an Iraqi pastor and I walked through the streets of a large metropolitan city in northern Iraq. I had been in the country for several days visiting Iraqi Christians and hearing their incredible stories of faith and courage. Now we were on our way to visit Nadim and his family, refugees from Najaf in southern Iraq who were new followers of Christ. I had met Nadim briefly at a worship service the day before, and I wanted to hear more of his story. I also hoped to find out if any other Muslim converts to Christianity were living nearby.

My friend and I headed up an alleyway that narrowed into a

dead end. Moments later, we stopped in front of a house surrounded by a crude metal fence. Hoping we were at the right location, my friend knocked on the gate leading into a small courtyard. An elderly lady with a weathered face stood behind a fence next door beating a tattered oriental floor rug that hung over a sagging clothesline.

She peered curiously at us, her eyes twinkling, and gestured toward the side of the house. Then she pointed to a small pathway that wound its way to the back of the building.

"You'll find them up there," she said in a rough voice.

Rusty metal stairs along the side of the building climbed to a second-story, nondescript concrete apartment. I didn't think anyone could live in such a place, but my friend assured me that the man and his family were waiting for us. Ascending the steps, we reached a landing typical of Middle Eastern dwellings. On the open rooftop, a simple plastic table and a few matching chairs sat in one corner; in the other corner lay a couple of thin sleeping mattresses. During the stifling summer months, most families who couldn't afford air-conditioning slept on the rooftops of their homes. A tattered plastic doll with blond hair lay on a set of cinder blocks near the mattresses. A little girl lived there too, it seemed.

Nadim appeared at the doorway, smiling as he welcomed us to his humble dwelling. "Please sit down," the young man said, gesturing toward a couple of plastic chairs.

His three children, including a little girl, scurried around on the rooftop. His wife quickly brought out a tray filled with bottled water, sodas, and pound cake.

As we sipped our drinks on the roof, Nadim shared his story.

"All my life I lived in Najaf, one of the holiest cities in the Shiite faith. Our home was less than five hundred meters from the main mosque, so I knew most of the major religious officials in town. In those days, like today, Najaf bustled with thousands of visitors who came from all around the world to worship and pray at the Imam Ali Mosque. I prayed there as well and was careful to observe all the religious practices of Islam.

"I had always been a faithful Muslim, but shortly after my wife and I married, I began to doubt my faith. I realized that many of the things I did were not expressions of true devotion to Allah but a facade to please my family and friends. In my heart I didn't believe anything I had been doing. Allah wasn't real to me at all.

"One day I decided to stop going to the mosque. I hardened my heart and ceased all my religious activities. I no longer believed in anything spiritual, and yet I still wanted to know Allah. My wife taught at a local university and came from a very large family—five sisters and four brothers—all devout followers of Allah. She sensed my struggle with my faith and with the teachings of the *mullahs*. She often encouraged me to go to the mosque and pray to Allah. When that didn't seem to help, she encouraged me to talk with the local imam. But that didn't help either. Finally she concluded that I was rebelling against the truth and ways of Islam.

"Soon my friends and family began asking me why I wasn't going to the mosque anymore. It was difficult to hide this from them, so I learned to avoid them by lying about when and where I went to pray. Yet in my heart, my desire to know the true and living God grew stronger. I knew there had to be more to being a Muslim than performing empty religious rituals.

"I had often heard religious men and preachers say that Allah was great, merciful, and compassionate. I believed that He was great, and I feared His almighty power. I also believed that doing His will was the ultimate purpose of my life. I knew many things about Allah, but I didn't *know* Him.

"In our town lived a very old man named Azam, who was a friend of our family. I had a deep respect for Azam and knew that he didn't go to the mosque either. He was the only one I could share my struggle with. So one day I went to visit him and told him about my despair and disillusionment with Islam. He listened quietly as I poured out my heart, and then he spoke about a man who transcribed the Holy Scriptures from Hebrew into Arabic.

"'If you will come back tomorrow, I will introduce you to this man,' Azam said.

"The following day I returned to Azam's house and entered a small room where Azam and another elderly man were talking. Flatbread and small cups of hot tea lay on a round wooden tray on the floor.

"'Please come in, Nadim,' Azam gestured. 'Allow me to introduce you to Ezra.'

"After greeting one another, Ezra asked me, 'Have you ever read the Bible?'

"I shook my head sadly and told him, 'In all my years in Najaf, I have never heard of such a book or met anyone who owns a copy.' Wondering if this Bible might contain what I was searching for, I asked, 'Where can I find this book?'

"Ezra gave me a penetrating look and then said, 'I will try to find this book for you, Nadim. It contains the answer to all your questions.'

"Two days later the old man came to my home with a small prayer carpet tucked under his arm.

"'*As-salaam aleikum, Nadim,*' he greeted me.

"'*Wa aleikum as-salaam,*' I replied.

"'I have a special gift for you,' Ezra said with a twinkle in his eye.

"Inviting him inside, I motioned for him to sit down. Ezra lowered himself gingerly onto a chair and then began to unfold the small carpet he had been carrying. A leathered old book slowly emerged from the folds of the carpet. Its pages were tattered and worn, and some of them fell to the floor. I stooped to gather up the fragile leaves of paper.

"Then Ezra said in a somber voice, 'Nadim, treasure this book as if it was water and bread. In it you will find life and the answer to all your questions about Allah.'

"Ezra placed the book in my hands and then rose to leave. As he shuffled out the door, I found myself unable to speak. Opening this strange book with trembling hands, I found my eyes irresistibly drawn to the words of a prophet named Matthew. As I began to read, the images I had of Allah leaped from the torn pages, and my heart began to burn. I believed that Allah was great and almighty. And now this book—the Bible—confirmed all that I had thought about Him. Yes, He was great, but He was so much more! For the first time I realized that I could know Him.

"The Koran taught that Allah was unreachable, unknowable, and untouchable, but the Bible said that I could really know Him in a personal way, that He was reaching out to me. Allah was alive, and He had found me! My heart burst with joy.

"That day I secretly began crying out to know the God of the

Bible. No one knew of my quest—not even my wife. I didn't know how to pray; I didn't know what to ask of Allah. I only knew that I was desperate for Him to show Himself to me and to teach me how to know Him. So that is what I prayed.

"Each day I feasted on more and more of Allah's words in the Bible and soaked in this new life I had been given. And yet all this time I was hiding my new identity from my family and friends. I wept and cried out to Allah every day, asking Him to pour Himself into my heart and help me know Him more. Little by little, I began to sense His presence and peace, even though I was alone in my faith.

"Soon this new life Allah had given me could no longer be contained. Like the new life that bursts forth when spring follows winter, Allah's Spirit burst forth in every part of my being. Through Allah's words, I came to understand that to truly know Him I needed to accept His Son, Jesus, or Issa, as He is called in my native tongue. As I opened my heart to Issa, I began to know Allah in a deeper way, and I knew I had to tell my wife about this miracle.

"Then one day over tea, I shared my innermost soul with her. She knew I had changed. As I recounted my story, her forehead tightened, and her eyes became dark. The moment I finished speaking, she stormed out of the kitchen in tears. 'You have denied your family and your faith!' she screamed. 'How could you? You have shamed us all!'

"I was crushed. I had assumed that she would embrace my newfound faith in the true God. The days that followed were dismal and discouraging. I so badly wanted my wife to believe, and I pleaded with Allah to change her heart and mind. But the harder I tried to explain my faith to her, the further away she seemed to drift from me. Despair threatened to overwhelm me as I realized she might never experience the joy and love I had discovered in Allah and His Son, Issa. I began to worry that in her anger my wife might tell her relatives that I had become a Christian, and that the local religious authorities would discover my secret. In spite of my fear, I trusted that God would take care of me.

"As my faith in Allah grew, I longed to find others who shared my beliefs. I could speak about God with Azam and Ezra, but I wanted to talk with believers my own age. I knew that revealing my conversion to just anyone would mean certain death, so one night I waited for my wife to go to sleep, and then I searched the Internet chat rooms and other social networks for people who wanted to talk about God. From that night on, I would go online after ten o'clock every evening and chat with people until the early hours of the morning.

"Soon I discovered others from my own city of Najaf who were asking the same questions I had been asking, but it was too dangerous to try to connect with them. Ironically, we were a secret Internet society of people searching for Allah in a city where millions of faithful Muslims came every year to find Him but never did.

"It was on the Internet that I began talking about my newfound faith in Issa. Taking on a different name to conceal my true identity, I found great joy communicating my decision to follow the God of the Bible. On the Internet, I became known as the Secret Disciple, and I soon found others with stories like mine. They had searched for Allah in Islam but had been disappointed to find that He was a distant, angry god, untouched by their hurts and struggles. And then, like me, they miraculously encountered the real God and were trying to find others who believed as they did.

"For many months, I continued chatting online with people searching for the true God. I often imagined that God Himself was sitting right next to me. Before long, I had connected with several followers of Issa, and we formed a small community of believers to encourage one another. Each night we secretly gathered in front of our computer monitors to talk about our faith and worship the God of the universe. We also linked to Christian Web sites that played worship songs in Arabic and sometimes broadcast special messages about Allah from other believers who had come out of Islam.

"One day, the conflict between my wife and me over my faith in Allah reached a breaking point. I was walking around the house reading the Bible aloud to her in the hearing of our children. When we entered our kitchen, she stopped and stood facing away from me. I could see her rigid body trembling. Then suddenly she turned toward me and angrily demanded that I choose either her and our children or the God I had found in the Bible. My knees became weak, and I flinched as if someone had stabbed me in the heart with a knife. Yet I immediately declared that I would choose the God of the Bible.

"My wife broke into a flood of tears. At first I thought she was weeping out of anger and despair, but then it dawned on me that God was melting her heart with His love. In an expression of humility and joy, she declared, 'I want to know this God you have found. He has changed you so much, and I, too, must know Him.'

"Filled with gratitude to Allah, I invited my wife to join me in this search to know Him and follow His plan for our lives together.

We encouraged each other in our faith and read the Bible together as we began to teach our children about the true God and His Son, Issa. We worried that our children might talk openly about what we taught them. We longed to share our faith with our families and friends, but we knew that if we did, we would endanger our children's lives as well our own. Afraid of the harm this would cause, we continued to live out our faith in secret.

"Perplexed about what to do, I e-mailed one of the Christian teachers I had been listening to over the Internet and shared my story with him. Concerned about our plight, he recommended that we leave Najaf and find a safer place to raise our children. He felt this was wise because we could learn more about God in a place where we had religious freedom, and I could attend Bible school to get training to serve God and reach my people with His love and truth.

"This man's advice seemed good to us, so like Joseph and Mary fleeing to Egypt with the baby Jesus, we sold all our possessions, left Najaf without telling our families or friends, and moved to this city. All of this happened just a few months ago.

"This move has been very difficult for us, and my wife and I have been unable to find work because of our ethnic background. We live on the money we made from selling our car, but those funds will run out soon. We applied for immigration to a foreign country, but when the officials saw our ethnic group on the paperwork, they denied us visas. We are trying to change our names for protection and to make it possible for us to get jobs, but this is also difficult to do in Iraq.

"My wife has suffered greatly since we left Najaf. Recently one of her sisters came to visit us and asked my wife many questions about why we talk to our children about the Bible and Issa. For the first time since her conversion, my wife shared her faith in Issa with her sister.

"In total disbelief and disdain, her sister condemned my wife's decision to forsake her religion and her family. 'We consider you dead!' she scoffed. 'You are no longer welcome as a family member!'

"None of my family knows about my faith yet, but I desire to return to Najaf to tell them and anyone else who will listen. I want to tell many in my hometown how God sought me out. He came looking for me, and He found me. Now I want to tell others of His great power to save. I want to use my skills in media and film to share God's love with my people. They will see God's great love for them if we tell them. I know the dangers are very real, and I could die for my faith. But I am ready to go. God will bring good out of Najaf!"

Nadim and his family continue to live in northern Iraq, where they attend a thriving church. Nadim is currently studying to be a pastor, and with his unique technology skills, he prays that he will soon be able to serve God through this medium, communicating the gospel with his people via radio and television, as well as other forms of media.

As an internally displaced person (IDP) in his own country, Nadim and his family know that if they return to Najaf, their lives will be in grave danger. Like Jesus' parents, who were forced to flee from Bethlehem to Egypt to escape King Herod's deadly wrath, Nadim's family has been forced to leave Najaf to escape certain death, and they are patiently waiting for God's timing to return home.

Nadim is sharing his faith by using the same technology that enabled him to learn more about God and connect with other believers—the Internet. With more than three hundred communications satellites circling the globe today, connecting via cell phones, high-speed Internet, and other electronic devices has become commonplace.

According to Internet tracking data, 1.7 billion people worldwide use the Internet, and from 2000 through 2009, daily Internet usage sky-rocketed a whopping 380 percent. In Africa alone, where Islam has gained a foothold, Internet use grew a staggering 1,392 percent! But as incredible as that statistic is, the Middle East has seen an even larger increase at more than 1,600 percent, even though this figure represents only 57 million users or 3.3 percent of Internet users worldwide. However, this significant increase in Internet use cannot be ignored. Ironically, one of the most oppressive regimes in the Middle East—the Islamic Republic of Iran—has seen an increase in Internet use of nearly 13,000 percent in the past nine years![1]

The rapid acceleration in global Internet connectivity has truly changed the world—especially the Middle East. Among closed Islamic countries, in particular, the Internet is fast becoming the primary means of sharing the gospel with Muslims in the twenty-first century. In many of these countries, the ability to connect to the Internet has opened up a gateway for young Muslims to learn about Jesus through an abundance of online Bible resources in English and many other languages.

The Internet has also unlocked the door for millions previously isolated behind the crescent curtain of Islam to engage in dialogue with followers of Christ around the world. Despite concerted attempts by oppressive governments and Islamic religious police to prevent their people from searching for the truth, many Muslims are still able to find the Bible online. Thanks to the Internet, God's Word is no longer chained (2 Timothy 2:9) but is increasingly accessible to all!

Audiovisual and digital technology have also made the Bible and various resource materials widely available to millions of illiterate people around the world, particularly in rural areas of Africa and Central Asia. Powered by small batteries, solar power, or small hand cranks, the audio Bible has become an incredibly effective tool in sharing God's Word and encouraging believers who can't read or write. The *Jesus* film in Arabic and other foreign languages has also had a powerful impact.

Another fascinating phenomenon that is gaining in popularity is discipling new believers long distance via the Internet. Several Christian organizations have begun to offer personal online discipleship to people around the world who want to know more about God. Google recently reported that more than twenty-one million people worldwide key the word *God* into their search engines every day. One well-known Christian ministry has responded to this apparent hunger to know God by launching an online social network to connect those who are searching for God with those who know Him. Through the wonders of technology, this network enables Christians in England to chat about Jesus with anyone online around the world, from the Andes of South America to the desolate reaches of Siberia to the overcrowded slums of India and the mountainous regions of Iraq and Afghanistan. If language creates an insurmountable barrier, the ministry can also connect a person who wants to chat online about God with a believer in his or her own country.

In the past few years, online social networks, such as Facebook and Twitter, have greatly expanded opportunities for worldwide communication. When my first book *No Escape from Grozny* was published, right away my teenagers told me I should set up a page on Facebook to let people know about it. Little did I realize that by doing so, I would receive a flood of messages from young Chechen refugees living in Jordan, Turkey, Russia, and Canada, who wondered how I knew about Chechnya and what I had done there. This social network immediately opened a new world for me to share my faith with others, and I have had repeated dialogue with several of these young people over the past few years.

Nadim's interest and expertise in various forms of media has put him on the cutting edge of sharing his faith in Issa with his own people in Najaf, Iraq, and with countless others throughout the Muslim world. He and his family are wonderful examples of how God is using human technology to shine His light into some of the darkest corners of the globe, especially the Middle East. The living God has no limits! He is able to reach anyone, anywhere, by any means—even the Internet!

Kurdish village life

David and Kurdish elder

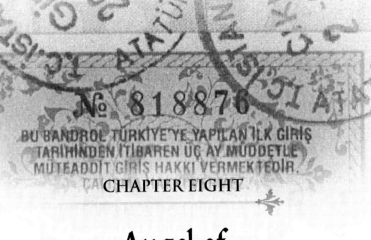

CHAPTER EIGHT

Angel of Baghdad

Istanbul and Yalova, Turkey; Baghdad, Iraq

A devastating earthquake struck northwest Turkey on August 17, 1999, reducing entire cities to rubble and causing unimaginable death and suffering. Hardest hit were Izmit, Adapazari, Gulluk, and Yalova. Thousands of people were trapped beneath tons of concrete and rubble, and many who survived the initial quake died hours later as powerful aftershocks continued to rock the region for several days. The quake left more than fifteen thousand dead and an estimated three hundred thousand homeless.

The death toll among the Kurdish and ethnic Christian populations was exceptionally high. Most were crushed or trapped inside cheaply constructed apartments built for those working in the Turkish oil industry. Folding like giant accordions, these buildings became concrete tombs for thousands.

I was deeply moved as I saw this tragedy unfold on CNN and other media outlets. Within hours I received a phone call from the director of an organization actively involved in assisting Kurdish refugees from Iraq and Turkey. Bob and I had met a year before and had a mutual desire to reach Kurdish people with the gospel.

"David, the earthquake has affected many Kurdish people and their families," Bob explained. "The hardest hit area is Yalova on the south side of the Strait of Bosporus. Two high-school buildings were destroyed, and we want to help rebuild these schools as a demonstration of God's love and care for the Kurds. They need this done quickly because the students are meeting outside in army tents right now. I'm leaving for Istanbul tomorrow. Do you want to join me?"

"When do we leave?" I said.

The next day Bob and I flew to Istanbul. Within an hour of landing, we were on a boat crossing over to Yalova to assess the damage. When we stepped off the boat and began walking through the city streets, I was horrified by the devastation. Mangled bed frames and splintered furniture lay crushed under massive piles of concrete, evidence of the sheer magnitude of the quake. Shreds of blood-stained clothes were strewn across broken electrical lines and utility poles. The stench of raw sewage hung heavily in the air. Turkish rescue teams were still searching for survivors, even though three days had passed since anyone had been found alive.

Bob and I moved on to the area where the high-school buildings had stood. Both of us were stunned. The buildings looked as if they'd been hit by an F5 tornado. As we wandered around the property, I saw pulverized schoolbooks, the remains of desks and chairs, a pencil here, a piece of blackboard there. It would take a miracle for these poor people to ever recover from such a disaster.

Bob and I agreed that we had to do something to help. On our flight back to the United States, we discussed how we could rebuild the high-school buildings and provide humanitarian aid to the earthquake victims.

The following day I began calling friends and pastors in the Philadelphia area, where we lived at the time. The response was overwhelming, and soon we had our team ready to go. It was mid-September when our team of twenty-eight volunteer construction workers boarded a jumbo jet heading for Istanbul, Turkey. The team was actually made up of financial accountants, postal workers, a fireman, a car salesman, a bank manager, and others unskilled workers. In reality, only two team members were qualified construction workers. One was a contractor and the other a stone mason.

After two weeks of backbreaking work, we accomplished what seemed impossible from the start: constructing two beautiful concrete tilt-up-style buildings that would soon become the new facilities for more than three hundred Kurdish and Turkish high-school students. Bob invited my family and me to return to Yalova two weeks before Christmas for the official opening and dedication of the new school buildings. We were excited to accept his invitation and felt it would be a perfect opportunity to bless the school children as well as earthquake victims with special Christmas gifts of clothing and school supplies.

Late one afternoon, as I was finishing up at the construction site, I heard a woman's voice and turned to see a middle-aged woman walking toward me, smiling as if she knew me. Although she wasn't wearing a head covering, she appeared to be from a Middle Eastern background, but a Muslim woman would never have been this forward.

Introducing herself as Malak, she asked if she could speak with me for a moment. I listened politely as she said she had heard that our group was in Yalova to help the earthquake victims. She had also heard that we might be returning soon with humanitarian gifts for children and Kurdish refugees.

"God willing, we'll be back for the school dedication in December," I said. "Why do you ask?"

She looked at me intently and replied, "God told me I could find you here. Can I tell you my story?"

Many times when people say things like this to me, I immediately throw up a defensive wall, anticipating some alien scenario. But this woman seemed different, and something told me I should listen to what she had to say.

"Of course I'd like to hear your story, Malak," I replied. "Is there someplace we could go to talk?"

"There is a nice little tea shop around the corner," Malak said with a smile. "There you can have a good Turkish tea and baklava while you listen."

I informed one of my team leaders at the construction site where I would be, and then Malak and I walked down to the tea shop. When we had settled down with our cups of tea, Malak began her story.

"Like many other Iraqis, my family and I fled our hometown of Kirkuk in the mid-1990s after the first Gulf War. Saddam Hussein blamed the Kurds and Christians for Iraq's troubles and incited terrible violence against us. My family and other Christians in Kirkuk had lived peaceably with our Sunni Muslim neighbors for many years, but during this time we began to suffer mistreatment and receive death threats. As the persecution against my family increased, we realized we were in grave danger.

"With the help of friends, we escaped to Istanbul, where we were given refugee status and political asylum. We are grateful to God for providing a refuge for us in this city, but life is very difficult. We have very few Iraqi Christian friends here, and most Turkish people look down on us because of our nationality. Even so, God has been faithful, and we feel He has called us to gather a small group of Iraqi believers together to encourage them and teach them God's Word."

Malak paused a moment and then smiled at me. "Would you like to come and see where we meet?"

"Of course," I said, returning her smile.

After I informed several team members of my plan and assigned one of them to get our group safely back to the hotel that evening, Malak and I set off for Istanbul. We walked together through the crowded streets of Yalova to the waterside docks, where a massive ferry—or water taxi—would transport us across the Bosporus to Istanbul. Spanning over a mile, the Bosporus is the main channel connecting the Black Sea and the Sea of Marmara. Funneling thousands of commercial ships each year through its waters, this channel is one of busiest shipping lanes on earth. Crisscrossing the

Bosporus multiple times every day, the water taxis connect Turkey's Asian and European sectors, providing transportation for passengers and commercial traffic.

When Malak and I arrived at the dock, hundreds of people were already boarding the water taxi—day workers returning home, business people, families, tourists, and missionaries. Soon after we boarded, workmen cast off the anchor lines, and the ferry slowly edged away from the dock. I stood beside Malak staring across the vast expanse of water and feeling a little awkward.

What in the world am I doing? I thought. *Here I am, a married man, traveling with a woman I just met an hour ago, who's taking me to some church somewhere in an Islamic city! There aren't any churches in Istanbul! And how could I leave my team behind? They'll get lost or kidnapped, and angry relatives will be demanding my head! I might even get kidnapped! How stupid can I be!*

Even though I was second-guessing my decision to go with Malak, in my heart I felt a tremendous peace that God had ordained our meeting and that I could trust her.

"Your team will be okay, David," Malak said, as if sensing my apprehension.

I smiled and then returned my gaze across the water. As I stared intently toward the west, Istanbul and its ancient mosques silhouetted the horizon. St. Sophia's church (now a museum) and the magnificent Sultan Ahmet Mosque—the Blue Mosque as it is affectionately called—stood as testaments of Istanbul's historic glory and prominence.

After the thirty-minute ride across the Bosporus, the huge ferry docked on the eastern side of Istanbul, the gateway to ancient Asia.

Although the ancient Ottoman and Turkish empires had long since died out, their influence lived on through the architecture of eastern Istanbul's ghettos.

It was almost six o'clock in the evening, and as the vestiges of daylight faded away, the Islamic call to prayer echoed from the minarets and loudspeakers of mosques buried among the hillsides of villages and small boroughs. As we walked through the narrow streets of the old city, we passed vendors peddling spices and copper vases. The air was heavy with the aroma of cumin and saffron. Whiffs of frankincense from Yemen and sweet tobacco from Egypt mingled with the earthy smell of freshly baked bread.

Although darkness was rapidly falling, I could easily discern the kind of structure that loomed before us. It seemed to be a very, very old church.

"Isn't this a Catholic church, Malak?" I asked, surprised.

"Yes, it is," she said with a slight smile on her face.

Walking up to the old wooden doors, Malak grasped one of the huge iron rings and slowly turned it. The heavy door creaked open, and we stepped inside. As my eyes adjusted to the darkness, I gazed in awe at the elaborate interior. It seemed that time had forgotten this small corner of the world. In classic Byzantine fashion, gothic overtones harkened back to the Dark Ages. The musty smells of candle smoke and incense permeated from the stone and wood. Gold-gilt altars and stained-glass windows enhanced the atmosphere of reverence and religious piety. For a moment I thought I heard Franciscan monks chanting.

Towering above everything else in the sanctuary were massive painted icons of the twelve apostles, Jesus, and Mary, each with halos over their heads. Yet these icons were different from any I had ever seen. At the bottom of each painted figure was a large inscription in Arabic, not Latin.

"These are the twelve apostles," Malak said. "This church was built over one hundred years ago. Isn't it remarkable how God knew that Iraqi people would be worshiping here and inspired the builders to write everything in Arabic so we could read the inscriptions?"

At that moment, I knew this lady was special and that God had indeed orchestrated our encounter.

"Malak, we will be happy to bring presents for your people in December," I said.

From that day on Malak became a true friend and sister in Christ.

A year after we first met in Yalova, I learned that Malak and her family had been granted refugee status in Canada and that they would be moving there soon. But we wouldn't see each other again until several years later…

When American troops invaded Iraq in 2003 and removed Saddam Hussein from power, lawlessness and violence erupted on the streets of Baghdad and in many other Iraqi cities. Sunni and Shia Muslims began settling old ethnic and religious scores, and ethnic Christians were caught in the middle. Those families who had money and opportunity fled to neighboring countries for asylum. Those who couldn't leave suffered through a living hell. Violence, ethnic brutality, and death became everyday realities in Baghdad. In spite of constant fear, believers clung to the Lord, trusting Him to protect them and provide for their basic needs.

As the war raged on, I often thought about Malak and her family, wondering how they were and whether she had returned to Kirkuk. Then one day, a friend told me that she was still living in Canada, and he gave me her phone number. When we spoke by phone a few days later, we reminisced for a while, and then Malak told me what God was doing among believers in Iraq. As I listened to their stories, I was amazed at their faith in the midst of a nightmare. I found Nasir and Fatima's story particularly moving.

Before the war, Nasir and his family lived near Sadr City in Baghdad. In their community, Orthodox Christians like Nasir and Fatima had always lived in relative peace with their Muslim neighbors in spite of their religious and ethnic differences. But the war changed everything.

When the bombing started, radical Shiite militia groups came into Nasir and Fatima's neighborhood and threatened their family. The couple wanted desperately to leave Iraq, but they had no money to pay smugglers, who charged up to five thousand U.S. dollars per person to help Iraqis escape across the border into Syria and Jordan.

One night a deafening burst of gunfire jolted Nasir and Fatima from their sleep. Fatima threw herself over their two young children to protect them, and Nasir ran downstairs to confront the intruders. Shouting "Death to Christians," several black-hooded men holding AK-47 assault rifles demanded money and forced the family to leave their home in the middle of the night. The gunmen fired weapons overhead as Nasir and his family hurried out of the house and ran down the darkened streets of Baghdad. Terrified and destitute, they sought shelter with another Christian family.

Sometime after this, Fatima was shopping at a local market when a suicide car bomber detonated his explosive device just one hundred meters away from her. The initial impact knocked her down, but she picked herself up and staggered over to help those who were injured. There, in pools of blood and smoking flesh, shredded bodies lay stacked like twisted sticks of wood. A young toddler, his face speckled with blood, sat crying next to his mother, her motionless body lying facedown on the ground. Fatima felt helpless...

After this experience, Fatima had nightmares, and her ears rang constantly. But she was thankful to be alive.

Malak went on to tell me about several Christian friends in the city of Mosul. After experiencing tremendous hardships and persecution during the war, they now lived in a constant state of fear and discouragement. Marginalized in a Muslim society, they were denied jobs that paid a living wage, making it all but impossible for them to provide for their families. Many were forced underground through intimidation, discrimination, and in some cases, outright physical persecution and death. In one bloody month of violence in October of 2008, many Christians were killed in Mosul, and their homes were burned to the ground in a frenzied rampage of radical Muslims.

Then in 2009, during a visit to Baghdad, Malak received a call from a friend at three o'clock one morning.

"Malak! Malak! They have taken our good friend Dr. Mahir!" Liza cried.

"What do you mean they have taken him?" Malak demanded.

"Today, in broad daylight! Right in front of our home! He was walking to his job at the hospital. We heard shouting coming from the street as a van pulled up alongside him. Several hooded men wearing Iraqi military fatigues jump out and tried to force him into the van. Pointing their automatic rifles at his head, they struck him repeatedly until he fell to the ground unconscious.

"When our next-door neighbor Omar ran out to help him, shots suddenly rang out. Omar slumped over and fell to ground, clutching his chest. The van sped away. We ran outside to help Omar, but it was too late. He lay motionless in a pool of blood, dead from the gunshot wound. What can we do, Malak?" Liza sobbed.

"We must trust God. He will help us," Malak said.

Two days later, Malak's phone rang again. It was Liza.

"Malak, the kidnappers have made contact with Dr. Mahir's family. They are demanding twenty-five phone books as ransom. (Twenty-five phone books is Iraqi street slang for twenty-five thousand U.S. dollars.) The family doesn't have that kind of money, and we don't have enough money to loan them."

"We are praying," Malak reassured her friend. "God is our only help!"

Several weeks went by before they saw Dr. Mahir again, alive. On the day Ramadan ended, his abusers dumped him, bruised and beaten, in front of the same house where he had been abducted. Malak prayed that by God's grace he would eventually recover as she reached out to help the family recover.

Into a netherworld of suffering and chaos, Malak—the Angel of Baghdad—wanders the bomb-cratered streets of Baghdad to care for people like Nasir and Fatima, Dr. Mahir, and many other internally displaced people (IDPs) who are suffering from the devastating effects of war, ethnic violence, poverty, and persecution. Malak touches literally thousands of Iraqi people in the name of Christ. No matter the dangers, she is the lifeline for many Christian families in Baghdad and beyond.

Over the years, I have continued to work with Malak as she serves the Lord and her people in Iraq and the Middle East. From our first encounter at a construction site in Yalova, Turkey, God destined us to share His love with those who suffer from the effects of war.

Malak tirelessly serves her people through acts of compassion, such as raising funds to purchase flour, oil, beans, sugar, and other necessary staples for families in need of food. She also provides much-needed medical assistance to those afflicted with cancer in Iraq—yet another deadly consequence of war. With war, the incidence of cancer has increased, but there is very little treatment available in the country.

Malak also encourages Christian women through vocational projects that give them a sense of worth. Among these successful business ventures are sewing projects for refugee women in Istanbul, Damascus, and Dohuk, in Kurdish northern Iraq. The women design and sew beautiful handbags, indigenous clothing, and many other accessories. The items are then brought to the United States and other Western nations to sell, and the proceeds are returned to the women's families. Projects like these instill a sense of worth, self-esteem, and a healthy attitude toward work in the women who craft the products. Those who purchase the creations are blessed as well and are reminded to pray for the spiritual and physical well-being of these refugees and their families.

The greatest gifts Malak brings to her people are her faith in the Lord, her spiritual encouragement and godly influence, and her tender care for the women in Iraq's Christian communities.

In war-torn countries throughout the Middle East, there always will be a need for angels like Malak, who bring hope, help, and healing in Jesus' name.

People often ask me how I feel about the war in Iraq. Was it right or wrong? Did I support it or not? Truth be told, my feelings about the war are mixed, but I would ask a far more important question: What are we doing as Christians to reach out with the hands and feet of Jesus to those who are suffering in the aftermath of such a horrible event?

Often when I speak at churches, I notice large displays of support for members of the U.S. military who are fighting in Iraq or Afghanistan. Sometimes letters from Congressmen and military commanders are posted on church bulletin boards, thanking members for their prayers and support. Pictures of men and women in their fatigues and combat uniforms hang in prominent places on walls of church foyers and vestibules.

Many support the members of our armed forces who are fighting on foreign soil and implementing U.S. foreign policy, but what about the tireless soldiers of Jesus all over the world, who are putting their lives on the line every day in the war for people's souls? Do we pray for them and support them as passionately as we support our troops, or do their pictures get stuck on some dusty wall close to the janitor's closet in the back of the church where nobody can see them?

Many gentle warriors for Christ serve in obscure and dangerous corners of the Islamic world, often in the same places where our armed forces are fighting. Some are Western missionaries whom God has called to serve in the Islamic world; others, like Malak, are natives of the Middle East who are reaching out in Jesus' name to their own people. Instead of the usual weapons of warfare, they wield weapons of the Holy Spirit as they face untold physical dangers and battle against the spiritual forces of evil pitted against them. They come as liberators of a different kind, holding out the good news of Jesus to a dying world. They offer God's love and real hope. And they urgently need our support!

In August 2009, National Public Radio (NPR) published an online commentary I wrote about my work with orphans and refugees in the war-torn region of Chechnya in southern Russia. A Christian going into such a dangerous and hopeless situation to share God's love, especially with Muslims (our supposed enemies), baffled the editor.

In a brief phone conversation the day the article was posted, she expressed to me her bewilderment.

"David, you are the most interesting Christian our people have ever heard of here at NPR. It amazes us in today's religiously polarized America to find a Christian who has a love for Muslims and wants to go to the places you go to just to tell them about your faith."

"That's exactly where you would find Jesus," I responded. "Where people need Him most. He wouldn't come as a peace negotiator, trying to broker a political deal to make everyone stop fighting. And He wouldn't come as a soldier or combatant, killing anyone who opposed Him. Instead, He would come as an angel of mercy, binding up those who have been ripped apart physically and emotionally by the devastating effects of war."

Wars and strife will never cease on this earth until Christ's return. That's the reality of the world we live in. Innocent people will continue to die in Baghdad from car bombs and improvised explosive devices (IEDs). Freshly dug graves will be filled with fallen soldiers and Islamic martyrs *(shahid)* from Iraq, Afghanistan, and other war zones. But as long as there are people like Malak—the Angel of Baghdad—there is hope!

Baghdad, Iraq

CHAPTER NINE

The Palestinians' Messiah

Muslim Quarter, Jerusalem

The warmth of the day faded into a cool evening. My friend and I walked down the narrow maze of streets that wound their way through the Old City of Jerusalem. Along the way, we had witnessed Hasidic Jews engaging in elaborate prayer rituals at the Wailing Wall and then hurrying home to begin their Shabbat (Sabbath).

In the doorways of shops, Muslim men in white head coverings (kaffiyeh) sat smoking copper pipes and drinking sweet tea. Foreigners, religious and nonreligious, were rushing from shop to shop, scooping up their last souvenirs before returning home to distant lands.

I had come to Jerusalem not as an American tourist—there are plenty of those—but as a pilgrim in search of answers, like millions who come to the Holy Land each year. Some pilgrims journeyed to the Holy City for the history, seeking to walk in the footsteps of Jesus; others came to convince themselves that He even existed. But my pilgrimage was different. I had come to experience a miracle: God's peace in Jerusalem and the fellowship of His people.

During my stay in the city, my friend Joseph invited me to join him and a group of Middle Eastern Christians who met each Friday evening in the Muslim Quarter of the Old City. Joseph had told me that many Palestinians were hearing the gospel and coming to Christ. Finding it hard to believe that Palestinians were worshiping Jesus in Jerusalem, I decided I had to see this unlikely phenomenon for myself!

My impression of Palestinians up to that point hadn't been very favorable. Like many Americans, I associated Palestinians with radical Islamic terrorism, Hamas, and the Palestinian Liberation Organization (PLO), not with biblical Christianity.

But that image didn't mesh with what Joseph had told me about the Palestinian believers we would be worshiping with that evening. I wondered what these believers thought of America…and what they would think of me. Would they perceive me the way many Arabs did: as a pro-Israeli, anti-Palestinian neo-Crusader? Would they treat me with hostility, or would they welcome me as a brother in Christ?

As we left the market area frequented by American tourists and made our way deeper into the Muslim Quarter, I could feel curious eyes following us—faces staring at us from darkened doorways, shadows creeping along the walls and the narrow alleyways of the Old

City. As an American, I felt conspicuous in such a neighborhood, as if I had neon lights over my head flashing "He's American! Rob him!" Apprehensive about what might happen if anyone disapproved of my presence, I tried to look as if I belonged there.

Nearby, I could hear the distinctive, haunting voice of the local *muezzin* calling faithful Muslims to the al-Aqsa Mosque for Friday evening prayers—the site where, ironically, the Jews believe that Solomon's temple once stood. On the distant Mount of Olives, the chimes from the Church of All Nations rang out. Listening to the chimes, I wondered if that evening I would witness what Jesus often talked about when He prayed: "[May] all of them be one, Father… so that the world may believe you have sent me" (John 17:21). Could it be true that Palestinians, Jews, and other Middle Easterners in Jerusalem were worshiping together as believers in Jesus? I prayed with all my heart that it might be so!

As we walked on, the street mysteriously opened into an ornate garden of an ancient church dating back to the Crusader period. Weathered stone walls lined the gravel pathway leading up to the entrance, and intricate iron arches were laced with sweet-smelling roses that perfumed the evening air. Barn swallows fluttered in a small fountain that accented the middle of the courtyard.

We entered the church through a wooden doorway and made our way up a narrow stone staircase into an expansive room. Cathedral ceilings towered overhead, with massive stone arches resting on granite pillars.

In the upper room, simple plastic chairs were arranged in a circle so that people could face each other. As Joseph and I took our seats, several of the men came over to greet us with hearty handshakes, their callous hands toughened by a lifetime of hard physical labor. Broad smiles stretched across their leathered faces, weathered by the sun and desert winds. From their hearts came the sweet Arabic greeting, *"Salaam!"* and other words of welcome.

One older man greeted me with the triple side-to-side kiss so commonly practiced in this part of the world, where men are men and emotions are openly expressed. Just as politely, women with olive skin and deep chestnut eyes smiled and nodded slightly to welcome us.

Suddenly, a man who appeared to be in his midthirties came and sat down next to me. With a huge smile, he said in perfect English, "Praise the Lord! It is great to have you join us tonight. My name is Mahmood, and I am a Palestinian believer from the West Bank. I will translate for you as you share God's Word."

Mahmood didn't look like a suicide bomber or a terrorist. He wasn't a Kalashnikov-toting fanatic wearing the green head band of Hamas, with "Holy Jihad" written in Arabic on his forehead. Mahmood was a brother, a Palestinian brother, excited to be a believer in Jesus Christ.

I relaxed and smiled back. I was among friends.

The evening began with music that was foreign to my ears and yet was so beautiful. The Middle Eastern believers had composed their own songs in Arabic, using musical styles unique to their culture. The minor keys and flowing melodies echoed off the cathedral ceiling. With no instruments, the a-cappella harmonies of this angelic choir sounded heavenly.

Looking around the room, I saw enraptured expressions on each face. Everyone seemed immersed in worshiping God. In contrast with so much of our Western-style worship that seems like glorified spiritual entertainment, that night I sensed a true spirit of worship, the presence of the Holy Spirit receiving our praise. I couldn't understand the language, but I didn't need to. It was so pure, so Christ-centered. For a moment I closed my eyes and wondered if this was what Pentecost must have sounded like. When I opened my eyes, I didn't see any tongues of fire hovering over worshipers' heads. There was no rushing wind—well, maybe there was, and I just couldn't see it. But it didn't matter; Jesus was there!

Just short of heaven, the singing and worship faded to silence. Mahmood prayed and welcomed me as a special friend from America. I briefly shared from the second chapter of Acts—not on the phenomenon of tongues or the outpouring of the Holy Spirit or the birth of the church, but rather about the people who comprised the early church. People from the Middle East, modern-day Islamic nations like Saudi Arabia, Libya, Syria, Iran, Iraq, Egypt, and Turkey, just to name a few. At Pentecost, people came from every nation under heaven and were amazed to hear the disciples praising God in their own languages. Now, two thousand years later, Jerusalem was once again the center of faith for all people—Jews and Gentiles.

It was surreal to teach from the Bible, with the very descendants of Abraham sitting before me—not only Palestinian Christians but believers from all over the Middle East. Looking into the face of a man from Iraq, I realized that Abraham probably resembled him in his younger days. Seeing the face of the apostle Paul (Boulos in Arabic) in one of the believers from Turkey wasn't at all far-fetched. In fact, if the Western-style clothing had been replaced with tunics and free-flowing robes, I would have thought I was in the Holy Land during Paul's time.

After our brief Bible study ended, the group was dismissed, but the smell of coffee and pastries invited us to linger and talk. In Middle Eastern culture, friendships are built, not manufactured. Time for food and conversation is essential. Life is all about relationships, not status or position. No drive-through fellowship here. No soccer or football games to rush off to. No important e-mails or calls to answer, no conflicting schedules to juggle. Just the simple breaking of manna—life itself.

Before I left the church, many of the believers thanked me for coming. One lovely Egyptian lady came over and said softly, "Please tell our brothers and sisters in America not to forget to pray for us. We pray for them every day. The next time you come, please bring more with you so we can pray and worship together."

That night in a small upper room in Old City Jerusalem, a group of Palestinian and Middle Eastern believers worshiped Jesus Christ as one family, where all the children were color blind, and race and religious heritage didn't matter. There were no barriers or borders, no security checkpoints, no passports, no castes, no politics or nationalities.

My quest was finally over; I had found the answer I was seeking: Palestinians are indeed worshiping Jesus in Jerusalem—and embracing Him as their Messiah!

Jews, Christians, and Muslims alike consider Jerusalem the spiritual center of the world. It's called the Holy Land, and yet throughout history, millions have been killed in the name of the God who supposedly dwells in the shrines, temples, and mosques in which the faithful so fervently worship. Even God's Son died a violent death in Jerusalem!

The Bible tells us to "pray for the peace of Jerusalem" (Psalm 122:6), but sadly, many who live there have experienced very little peace. Violence and death are woven into the history of this part of the world. It's an inescapable fact. But life and hope are also part of Jerusalem's heritage.

Jerusalem was not only the birthplace of the Christian faith, but it's also where God first poured out His Spirit on believers (Acts 2). Jesus' death on a Roman cross was only part of the story. God saved the best part for last: Jesus was raised to life in Jerusalem, and someday He will come back in glory to "bring salvation to those who are waiting for him" (Hebrews 9:28), including untold numbers of Palestinians who have accepted Him as their Messiah.

But let's face it, when most Americans hear the word *Palestinian,* we don't think of Christians. We tend to think of radical Islamic groups like Hamas and the PLO. We think of suicide bombers from refugee camps in the West Bank, young Palestinian men throwing rocks at Israeli soldiers, and masked extremists launching Katyusha rockets at Israel from rooftops in Gaza City. And we think of "the Wall," the giant concrete barrier cordoning off portions of the West Bank to protect the Israeli people from Palestinian terrorists who want to annihilate them. The Wall is a fortress, a haven against attack.

But the vast majority of Palestinians I have met over the years aren't suicide bombers or rock throwers or masked extremists with rocket launchers. For them, the Wall is a prison, locking them into a never-ending cycle of despair and poverty, punishing all Palestinians for the actions of extremists.

The Western media often presents only one side of the story. The side we don't see is that most Palestinians are decent, hardworking people who just want to live in peace. They have hopes and dreams for their children that don't involve jihad or suicide bombing. Like the believers I met in the Muslim Quarter of the Old City, many Palestinians long to know the living God and are searching for His truth.

Many churches in the West support and encourage Messianic believers in Israel, and I rejoice to see our Jewish brothers and sisters come to Yeshua as their Messiah! But my heart breaks when I see the Western church fail to recognize and support Palestinian believers. This is one of the greatest injustices I see in the church today. Like Messianic Jews, Palestinian believers desperately need our prayers and encouragement.

More than once I have heard the lament of Palestinian Christians: "Why do the American Christians spend billions of dollars a year to come to the Holy Land and support Israel, and yet they won't come and visit us in the West Bank as well? Are we not as much a part of the body of Christ as Jewish believers? We worship the same God and believe in the same Jesus they do. We need people to pray for us and not forget us behind this wall of concrete!"

Their question deserves an answer. I believe that fear, distrust, and an overwhelmingly negative perception of Palestinians have caused us to close our eyes and hearts toward them. In our fight against Islamic extremism, we all too often lose sight of the people themselves. People just like us, whom Christ died to save. Fueled by a constant drumbeat of voices warning us about Islam and its plans to destroy or take over America, hatred can easily take root in our hearts, crowding out the love and forgiveness God calls us to show to *all* people, even our enemies. Horrific images of the terrorist attacks on 9/11 are seared into our minds, making it almost impossible to view Muslims as anything but killers.

In spite of all the reasons we might have to fear and despise the Palestinian people, and indeed all Muslims, God is calling us to surrender any fear or prejudice in our hearts and to seek a biblical perspective of the world we live in. Jesus Himself is our peace; He has "destroyed the barrier, the dividing wall of hostility" between Jew and Gentile (Ephesians 2:14). What a powerful, life-changing realization this is! If we truly let the love and peace of Christ rule in our hearts (Colossians 3:14-15), how might this change the way we see Muslims and interact with them? How many more Palestinians might come to Christ through our witness?

In that tiny upper room in Jerusalem, I saw a glimpse of heaven, where all nations and races, Jews and Gentiles will worship Jesus together with one heart. The dividing walls of fear and hatred will be torn down for all eternity, and God's people will radiate His love, joy, and peace!

"The Wall" - West Bank - Bethlehem

"The Wall" - West Bank - Bethlehem

CHAPTER TEN

Wall of Tears

Jerusalem and the West Bank

A rush of emotions surged through me as I gazed from the Mount of Olives toward the limestone walls of Jerusalem. The Eastern or Golden Gate—one of the city's most recognizable landmarks— glistened in the early morning sun. I was mesmerized. I couldn't believe that I was about to visit one of the most hallowed and disputed pieces of land known to modern man.

Descending the dusty path through a grove of gnarled olive trees with roots that twisted like snakes across the ground, I joined a tapestry of humanity slowly plodding toward a spiritual destiny. Like thousands of religious pilgrims before us, we were drawn to the holy city like moths to a flame. Eastern Orthodox priests, Roman Catholics, and religious locals were all easily identified by their black robes and religious hardware. Hasidic Jews stood out from the rest, with their traditional black hats, long strands of curly hair dangling from beneath their yarmulkes (skullcaps), and small leather prayer boxes (phylacteries) on their foreheads. And then there were the Holy Land tourists—Americans, Europeans, Asians—wearing T-shirts and Bermuda shorts, with cameras hanging around their necks. The New Yorkers were easy to recognize with their Yankees baseball caps displayed proudly on their heads. Whether saints or sinners, we were all intent on one thing: connecting with God, each in our own way.

Climbing out of the rock-strewn valley below the Mount of Olives, I could see our destination in the distance: the Western Wall, or as it's more commonly known, the Wailing Wall or Wall of Tears. Ever since the Romans destroyed Jerusalem in AD 70, Jews have come to this wall to worship, weep, and pray. Ironically, on the other side of the wall, on the former site of the Jewish temple, lay the brilliant al-Aqsa Mosque, where thousands of Muslims worship Allah.

We quickened our pace, walking up the road leading to the Dung Gate, the most frequently used entrance for visiting the Wailing Wall and the Temple Mount. As its name implies, the Dung Gate was the millennia-old portal through which trash and other waste was transported out of Jerusalem.

As we approached the gate, I sensed excitement and anticipation sweeping through the crowd. Pressing forward through the ancient entryway, elderly Jewish men began to cry "Shalom! Shalom to you, O Jerusalem!" with tears streaming down their wrinkled faces. When we reached the wall, Catholics knelt and crossed themselves while tourists inserted paper prayers and notes into the cracks of the massive stones alongside thousands of other prayers.

Sounds of wailing rose from worshipers as Orthodox Jews bobbed and rocked back and forth in an elaborate prayer ritual. Other visitors wandered through the crowd snapping pictures. I was amazed at the sincerity and religious diversity of those who had come to pray and worship.

In stark contrast to the lament at the wall, joyous celebrations were taking place in other corners of the square. In festive fashion, young Jewish boys ceremoniously passed from childhood to manhood as they recited passages from the Torah during their bar mitzvah rituals. Separated from the men and boys by waist-high, curtained barriers, the women threw candy and danced in traditional Jewish circles.

Watching the religious fervor of the Jews at the Wailing Wall reminded me of the people I had yet to meet.

After lingering at the wall for an hour or so, I walked several meters to the entrance of the Temple Mount. Unlike the entrance to the Western Wall, this tiny gate was heavily fortified with barbed wire, metal detectors, German shepherd guard dogs, and riot police, along with Israel Defense Forces (IDF) soldiers manning fifty-caliber machine guns behind concrete barriers.

An entirely different scenario was unfolding on this side of the wall. Few people were waiting in line to enter this part of the city. Not that I blamed them. The IDF soldiers were very intimidating.

"Are you Jewish?" one Israeli soldier asked in a rough voice as he peered at me from behind dark sunglasses.

"No, I'm an American," I replied.

"Figures!" he said in disdain. "Only an American would want to come up here."

After the soldier questioned me for a few tense moments and searched my camera bag, he allowed me to pass. Inside the gate, on the opposite side of the Wailing Wall, another pilgrimage was taking place. Thousands of devoted Muslims were gathering for Friday prayers on the vast plateau of the Temple Mount near the al-Aqsa Mosque. Next to the mosque stood the famous Dome of the Rock, which, according to Muslim tradition, sits on the rock where Abraham willingly offered to sacrifice his son Ishmael in obedience to God.

Just like the worshipers on the far side of the wall, Israeli Arabs from eastern Jerusalem; Jordanians from Amman; refugees from Gaza and the West Bank cities of Bethlehem, Hebron, Jericho, and Ramallah; and Muslims from distant parts of the world had traveled to Jerusalem with one goal in mind: to connect with God. But on this side of the wall, the scene was much more subdued. Old and young men alike sat side by side at a fountain, washing their forearms and feet in the cool water to ritually purify themselves before corporate prayer. Woven tapestries and ornate carpets adorned the grounds outside the mosque, where worshipers would kneel to pray.

When I approached one of the officials posted at the door, he gave me a stern look.

"May I enter the mosque?" I ventured.

"You are a foreigner. Are you Muslim?" the man said.

"If you're asking if I am in submission to Allah—since that is the literal Arabic translation of *Muslim*—then yes, I am."

"Then you may observe prayers today, and if you wish, you may enter the mosque," he said, smiling. "Please remove your shoes and wash your hands and feet."

As I performed these Islamic purification rituals, I recalled the account in Exodus 3 when God told Moses to remove his sandals on holy ground, and the passage in Psalm 24, when King David wrote that anyone wanting to approach God must have clean hands (figuratively speaking, of course) and a pure heart.

After washing, I placed my shoes in a designated area near the fountain, along with thousands of other shoes and sandals. Moving to the rear of the crowd, I quietly stood in the shade of a tree while the throng assembled in mass. When the *caliph* (spiritual leader) signaled the beginning of prayers, worshipers knelt in perfect unison, bowed, and then touched their foreheads to the carpet. I watched in awe as thousands of Muslim men expressed their reverence and devotion to Allah.

That October afternoon, as the sun drifted toward the western horizon, I realized that on both sides of the Western Wall, people of faith were trying their best to connect with God, crying out to the One they desperately wanted to know. And yet God's heart was breaking because another wall separated them from Him—a man-made wall of rigid religious systems and dogmatic ideologies created to force God into their myopic world of understanding.

Although I was impressed with the devotion of Jews and Muslims alike, I realized that the rituals they so passionately and faithfully performed to draw closer to God were devoid of life. They were reaching out for God, but most of them had never experienced a real relationship with Him. And the wall that separated them from the living God was also separating them from one another.

In May 2006, I returned to the Holy Land to visit friends in Bethlehem. I quickly discovered that Israel now had two Western Walls: the ancient Western Wall I had visited in 1979 and a new security wall surrounding the West Bank. The Wailing Wall was still packed with pilgrims inserting paper prayers into the cracks and crevices. Hasidic Jews were still bobbing and reciting prayers from their pray books. Eastern Orthodox priests and Roman Catholics were still there too, along with all the tourists taking pictures.

But as my taxi left Jerusalem en route to Bethlehem, I noticed a new twenty-five-foot concrete wall snaking ominously through the bleak Judean hillside. It resembled a gray python, winding, curling, wrapping itself around its prey.

Israel began constructing this security barrier—likened to the Berlin Wall and the Great Wall of China—on June 16, 2002, as a temporary deterrent to keep terrorists from slipping into Israel from the West Bank and killing innocent civilians on the streets of Jerusalem. Years later, the wall, extending 750 kilometers along the West Bank, looked anything but temporary to me.

No paper prayers were inserted in the cracks of this wall. In fact, no sensible person dared to come near it for fear of being electrocuted or even shot. Equipped with thermal-imaging systems, video cameras, electric sensors, sniper towers, and machine guns, the concrete fortress discouraged anyone from approaching. And yet, in a show of defiance, the drab gray concrete had been colorfully decorated with graffiti. I suspected it was the handiwork of young Palestinian Picassos armed with a stony will and spray paint. Some of the messages were angry and bitter, revealing the deep-seated rage that many Palestinian youth harbor against the Israeli government. Other messages radiated peace and hope, revealing the longings of most Palestinians to live in harmony with their neighbors. Hope and despair etched on the surface of a wall separating Israelis and Palestinians, keeping them from coming together so they might understand and learn from one another.

As I gazed at this towering barrier, a heartbreaking realization struck me: This was the Palestinians' Wailing Wall. For thousands of innocent Palestinians living in Israel and the West Bank, this wall had brought nothing but tears and sorrow. It had locked them in a prison of despair and poverty, denying them the ability to sell produce farmed on their own land and restricting access to schools, workplaces, clean water, and medical services.

Slicing into Palestinian territory like a giant scar, the wall unilaterally redrew political borders, facilitating the expansion of Orthodox Jewish settlements while trapping the Palestinian people in an overcrowded cesspool of squalor. Although I understood the Israeli justifications for the wall, I was outraged at such apparent injustice against innocent Palestinians.

I longed to cross that barrier and talk with the Palestinian people. I wanted to see for myself how they really lived and who they really were. But the wall that kept Palestinians inside the West Bank also kept Westerners like me outside. Travel restrictions made it all but impossible for Westerners to visit, but fear, mistrust, false stereotypes, and misinformation also erected walls in our hearts.

I knew that Palestinian Christians were living behind that concrete wall, suffering under deplorable living conditions. I longed to encourage them and let them know that other believers were praying for them and hadn't forgotten them. I also wanted so desperately to reach out to the thousands of Palestinians who had yet to hear about the living God who loved them and sent His Son to free them from sin and despair. They, too, needed to know Christ as their Messiah.

Continuing on toward Bethlehem, I noticed that the IDF checkpoint between Bethlehem and Jerusalem was exceptionally busy that afternoon. Hundreds of Palestinian employees were returning home after a day's work in Jerusalem. The exhaust fumes from dilapidated Mercedes Benz automobiles were nauseating.

An Israeli soldier methodically examined the car ahead of ours, tapping the side panels and listening for any sounds that might indicate hidden explosives. The soldier then extended a mirror underneath the car to check for explosives as well. A German shepherd sat at attention, his eyes fixed intently on those crossing the checkpoint on foot. Soldiers checked each worker's permit and identity papers for authenticity. I was reminded again how deeply ethnic hatred and distrust separates people.

I glanced over at a prominent sign that read "NO JEWS PERMITTED PASSAGE."

How ironic, I thought. Jesus himself would have been forbidden to visit the city of his birth. Then again, things hadn't changed much in two thousand years. Joseph and Mary weren't welcome in Bethlehem either.

"Identification papers, please," demanded a young female security officer sitting behind bulletproof glass.

At first, my blue American passport didn't seem to be a problem.

Then, as if an alarm went off in her head, the puzzled officer stared at me in disbelief.

"Mr. LeCompte, do you realize it is dangerous for an American to visit the West Bank?" she asked.

"Yes, I do realize it's dangerous, but I will be among friends—Christian friends," I answered politely.

Apparently satisfied with my response to her brief psychiatric evaluation, she asked where I was going and why I had come to the West Bank.

"To spend the afternoon with a special family in Bethlehem," I replied.

The security officer finally returned my passport and waved us through the gate. Free from the tensions encountered at the IDF checkpoint, my Arab driver burst into song as our taxi sped toward Bethlehem. After a fifteen-minute drive through the Judean hillside, the town of Bethlehem came into view. Contrary to the well-known Christmas carol about Bethlehem, it was anything but a little town. Buses were crammed into Manger Square like sardines, waiting for tourists to return from afternoon mass at the Church of the Nativity and the Shepherds' Fields nearby.

Aggressive street vendors peddled intricate olive-wood carvings of the nativity scene and the crucifixion of Christ. Dove ice-cream bars, Coca-Cola, and Pepsi were also on sale. Gold and silver glistened under intense lights from myriad fine jewelry shops that lured shoppers off the streets. Like the night Jesus came to earth, Bethlehem was busy.

As my driver maneuvered the taxi down the narrow streets, I thought about my friend Wahdi and his family. After the second

Palestinian Intifada erupted on September 28, 2000, Wahdi, his wife, Safa, and their five daughters were forced to flee their humble home in Gaza and move to Bethlehem as refugees. Wahdi had struggled to find housing for such a large family, but in time they settled into the community, established a small business, and gained the respect of their Muslim neighbors.

When my taxi pulled up in front of a modest home, I realized I had arrived at my destination. The air was filled with the distinct aroma of meat cooking on an open grill. Inhaling deeply as I stepped out of the car, I paid the driver and then made my way to the door.

While I waited for someone to answer my knock, I soaked in the tantalizing smell of grilled meat. Moments later, Wahdi greeted me at the door, a huge smile on his face.

"Please come in," he said in broken English. "Come with me to the balcony. I am cooking kabobs. I have lamb, beef, and even a special surprise for you, my American guest—pork kabob!"

"Pork?" I asked in surprise. "Aren't West Bank stores owned by Muslims?"

Wahdi burst into laughter. "Yes, brother. But we are Christians. I get the pork from friends who work for the American embassy in Jerusalem. Anything is available if you know who to contact."

Humbled by Wahdi's hospitality and spontaneous joy, I slipped off my shoes and stepped inside the house. The kitchen was bursting with festive excitement. Wahdi's wife, Safa, flitted about, directing her daughters with the precision of an air-traffic controller. Dish after dish of ethnic food flooded the dining table. Fresh dolmas (wrapped grape leaves stuffed with rice and meat), green onions, hot skewers of lamb and beef—and, oh yes, pork.

As we enjoyed food and fellowship that evening, sharing our hearts and lives with one another, my heart overflowed. What an incredible bond we had in Christ!

That evening, as our visit drew to a close, Wahdi implored me to stay. Though I longed to spend more time with my friend and his family, I knew how dangerous it would be for them. Local police intelligence would already have been informed of my visit, either by the taxi driver or through official IDF channels. An American staying overnight with a Palestinian refugee family from Gaza wasn't wise. We both knew I had to leave.

With tears in his eyes, Wahdi said, "David, we are so happy you came to visit us. So many Christians come to Israel to see the Holy Land where Jesus walked. What we can't understand is why they don't come to see us too. Do they not know there are Palestinian believers here? Do they not care about our plight? We feel forgotten…neglected. We realize the new security wall makes travel between Bethlehem and Israel difficult, but we need fellowship and encouragement. Please let your friends know that we wait for them to come and see us."

Echoing the voices of Palestinians in the previous chapter, the questions and feelings of abandonment my friend Wahdi expressed have haunted me since that day in Bethlehem. Why don't Christian tourists reach out to Palestinian believers during their visits to the Holy Land? According to the Israeli Ministry of Tourism, more than

1.8 million Christian tourists visited Israel in 2008, with one million pilgrims visiting West Bank towns like Bethlehem and Nazareth. And yet very few Christian tourists ever take the time to visit their brothers and sisters in Christ who live in these towns.

Western Christians are largely unaware that God is moving among the Palestinian people in the West Bank and the Gaza Strip. And yet a vibrant community of Palestinian believers has emerged in these conflict-ravaged, impoverished areas. As this community increases in numbers, believers are becoming bolder, risking their lives to share their faith in Jesus with fellow Palestinians. But they desperately need our prayers and support. That's why I continually encourage church groups visiting the Holy Land to add a day or two to their trip so they can spend time with Palestinian believers.

I realize that the security situation is a factor, but that can't be the only reason why Western believers aren't reaching out to Palestinian Christians. I often wonder whether Western believers are simply unaware of their Palestinian brothers and sisters in Christ, or worse, whether they are disinterested, indifferent, or even prejudiced against them. Whatever the reasons, I hurt for Wahdi and other Palestinian believers, who remain separated from the body of Christ not only by a towering security wall but by invisible barriers of fear, distrust, and racial hatred.

Spending time with Wahdi made me more convinced than ever that the Christian church in America must hear the stories of Middle Eastern believers. Western Christians know about the Jewish Wailing Wall, but do they know about the Palestinian Wall of Tears?

Two thousand years ago, Jesus died on a cross in Jerusalem, tearing down the wall that separated all of humankind from God.

But in the Holy Land today, walls continue to separate people, culturally, racially, and spiritually. A gigantic security wall—an ugly scar defacing the land—divides Jew from Palestinian, both Abraham's descendants. And yet behind this wall, God is transforming lives. Imposing though it may be, a wall can't stop the good news of Jesus from reaching the Palestinian people. God will always find a way to communicate His incredible love and grace to them!

Ramallah – West Bank, Israel

Western Wall – Jerusalem

CHAPTER ELEVEN

The Ramallah Teahouse

Ramallah, West Bank

On a cool day in the fall of 2005, I joined a handful of colleagues on a day trip to Ramallah, the capital city of the West Bank, bordering Israel. Known for its life and vigor, Ramallah also bore ugly scars from the Second Palestinian Intifada or "shaking off" of the Israeli occupation of the West Bank that took place in the year 2000. Arabic graffiti on the giant security wall surrounding the city reminded the world that memories of the occupation were fresh among the Palestinian people, and the embers of resistance still smoldered just under the surface of everyday life.

Ramallah wasn't a typical tourist stop for most Americans, but we had heard of a small group of Palestinian university students holding Bible studies in a teahouse just outside the city and were curious to see it for ourselves. After being questioned at several IDF checkpoints, our taxi crossed over from Israel to the West Bank, separated by a massive concrete wall.

On the outskirts of the city, years of neglect were evident everywhere, a tragic legacy of Yasser Arafat's government. Broken street lights dangled from their mountings, their wires stripped by copper thieves. Trash littered the roadsides, and gangs of young men loitered on street corners smoking cigarettes and playing cards. With unemployment in the West Bank near 28 percent and more than 59 percent of the population living below the poverty level, the Palestinians were struggling to find hope for their future.

We soon arrived at the central taxi station near the renowned Times Square of Ramallah, named for its resemblance to the famous New York City landmark, only much, much smaller in scale. The main intersection in town, the square was a hangout for locals to watch the overly animated traffic police entertain the masses and direct the chaotic flood of traffic navigating the roundabout every day.

Wanting to experience the sights, sounds, and smells of the city, we paid our taxi driver and then took a leisurely stroll down the maze of city streets. Ramallah was pulsating with life. Marinated lamb and chicken roasting over open fires permeated the air with a tempting aroma that competed with the smell of fresh *lavash* (Palestinian flatbread) emanating from storefront bakeries. A block later we stepped into a small coffee shop, the local version of Starbucks, for a good strong cup of coffee.

After ingesting enough caffeine to last us for days, we ventured back out onto the main street. Vendors peddled their wares in open-air markets, selling everything from bananas to large sacks of pistachios, almonds, and cashews, to the latest Siemens cell phones. Freshly slaughtered animals—chickens, goats, sheep—hung from wire racks.

Several little boys with dirty faces and ragged clothes spotted us and came running. Like bees swarming around a hive, they tugged at our pants, pleading for us to buy packs of chewing gum and candies from them. Within minutes, we became the Pied Pipers of Ramallah. It was time to leave. We had another more compelling reason for coming to the West Bank.

We walked quickly back to the taxi station, where a shark pool of frenzied taxi drivers instantly surrounded around us, hoping for business from venerable Americans with U.S. dollars.

"Taxi, mister? I make good price! What you want to pay? I make special price just for you!"

"My taxi, mister! I make best price!"

"I speak good English, mister! I have brother in Chicago! I like America! My name Fadi. You like my taxi, mister!"

I wondered which was worse—the little boys or the cab drivers.

With the fare negotiated, we grabbed Fadi with the brother in Chicago, piled into his little Opel taxi, and sped away from the downtown square in a swirl of dust and exhaust fumes.

"Where you want to go? Jerusalem?" he shouted with a big smile.

"No, we want to go toward Nablus," I said.

The taxi driver's face turned ashen white. "Nablus? Are you crazy?" Fadi shouted. "We can't go there!"

"No, no! We don't want to go *into* Nablus, just toward it," I corrected, handing Fadi a small piece of paper with an address scribbled on it.

"That is good, my friend! I was about to turn around and let you hire another taxi. Don't get me wrong. I like America! But if I take you in my taxi to Nablus, well, the al-Aqsa Martyrs would cut all our throats." Fadi burst out laughing as he drew a finger across his neck. "Don't worry! Ramallah is my town. You are safe here," he assured us.

We left the downtown area heading north on a small road. Just outside the city, we came upon a small stone building tucked into a rock-strewn hillside. Crudely constructed out of rough field stones, with a thatch roof and a few small windows with wooden shutters, the little stone structure didn't look like much. But a brightly colored sign out front spoke a message of life and hope: Ramallah Teahouse. What a contrast to the hopeless, hate-filled graffiti emblazoned on the walls of the city.

Following a well-worn path, we approached the teahouse. I knocked on the small wooden door and waited with my companions in nervous anticipation.

When the door opened, a young woman looked out at us expectantly. "Please come in, my friends," she said with a smile.

I ducked my head through the low doorway and stepped into an open, almost cavelike room. I felt as if I had traveled back in time. The room was brightly lit with hundreds of candles, and the aroma of frankincense filled the air. In one corner of the room was a small table surrounded by piles of pillows and carpets. Books and magazines—some in English and others in Arabic—lined the recessed stone bookshelves along the walls, and several computers with Internet connections sat nearby.

"Please make yourselves comfortable," the young lady said, gesturing toward the pillows. "My name is Hanifah. I will go now and prepare tea for you. It is our way of saying we are blessed to have you as our guests. We want those who come to Ramallah Teahouse to feel they are welcome and that they can find peace and fellowship here."

"My name is David," I replied with a smile. "My friends and I heard about your group here, and we've come to see what it's like to be a follower of Jesus Christ in Ramallah. We're happy to meet you as well."

Hanifah smiled shyly and then excused herself, disappearing into another room.

When we had taken our seats on the floor, two dark-haired young men joined us at the table.

"Welcome to Ramallah Teahouse! I am Rafi," one of the men said with a radiant smile.

In traditional Middle Eastern style, tea was served in little glasses as we leaned back against huge plush pillows. Small pieces of baklava and traditional Arabic sweets sat on a tray in front of us. I knew from experience that the tea would be piping hot and the sweets would be really, really sweet. So to avoid burning my tongue, I took a small bite of the baklava first and then sipped the tea *very* slowly.

"Hanifah told us that you are Christians and that you have come to talk to us about life here in the West Bank as believers," Rafi began. "We are happy that you have come, but I must say that I am somewhat surprised as well. Very few Westerners know there are Palestinian Christians in the West Bank, and even fewer would take the risk you have to travel here to meet us face-to-face. We understand how dangerous it is for you to come here." Rafi paused before adding with a smile, "But now that we have drunk tea and eaten baklava together, we are true brothers!"

We chatted casually for a few minutes and then Rafi's expression became serious. "I will tell you now what you came to learn from us. Many young people live here in Ramallah. Most are Muslim, but a number of us come from Orthodox Christian backgrounds, since our parents and grandparents were Christians. Even though Islam is the dominant religion in the West Bank, a growing number of young people have become converts from Islam. For this we are experiencing many troubles at the hands of Muslim radicals, who accuse us of brainwashing their children.

"But the local Palestinian officials like us because we provide the young people with a place to have clean fun. For many university students, our teahouse offers them another place where they can study and socialize with their friends, and some students even come here to use our Internet risk free. You see, most of the Internet cafés in the city are owned by Muslims and are closely monitored by the radical religious police from the mosque. Since we are Christians and we have our own servers, the students trust us more and are not afraid to use our computers.

"The Palestinian Authority, which is secular and more political, also sees us as a positive influence that keeps young men from being recruited into radical Islamic factions. We pay a great price for this work, though. Come! I will show you what some in Ramallah think of us."

Rafi led us into a small burned-out room on the lower level and gestured toward the blackened walls. A firebomb had been thrown through a window, and the intense flames had consumed a computer and a number of books that had been in the bomb's path.

"This happened several weeks ago," Rafi said. "The police have investigated, but no one has been arrested. After the fire, the local mosque warned us that if we don't close our teahouse, we will suffer more persecution. At first, fear came into our hearts, but after we prayed, we sensed God giving us the strength to stand strong. The eyes of Ramallah are watching to see if we will cave in to the extremists' demands. Some of our neighbors have come by to encourage us, and an elderly Muslim man even stopped by the other day to tell us to defy the radicals.

"We feel stronger today because we have remained faithful to God. And other young people in Ramallah are taking courage and becoming bolder because of our stand. God has honored our obedience, and because of this, more young people are coming to our teahouse to learn about Jesus. Our teahouse is a safe haven in Ramallah. It creates a pleasant environment for young people to gather, have good tea, and form friendships. It also gives us many opportunities to share our faith in Jesus and talk about the Bible.

"We hope you are encouraged to see what God is doing here among our people and that you will tell others in America what you have seen and heard. Please let your friends know that not everyone in the West Bank is a suicide bomber. Most of all, remember to pray for us...and don't forget that Jesus is a big fan of our tea and baklava," Rafi concluded with a huge smile.

The sun was already low in the western sky as we said our good-byes to Rafi and Hanifah at the little teahouse that afternoon.

As our taxi made its way back to Jerusalem, the sweetness of our fellowship with these two Palestinian believers warmed my heart. Staring into the setting sun, I heard Rafi's words echoing in my thoughts: "Let your friends know that not everyone in the West Bank is a suicide bomber. Most of all, remember to pray for us!"

Many Westerners are surprised to learn that Ramallah—literally translated "height of God"—was founded as a Christian community in the mid-1500s by the Hadadeen tribe, who were descendants of Yemenite Christian Arabs.[1] Over the centuries, Ramallah grew into a major agricultural community attracting mostly Christian farmers and sheepherders from many regions of the Middle East.

In the early 1800s, the predominately Christian community built both a Greek and an Arab Orthodox church for their followers. Then around the middle of the century, the Catholics, Episcopalians, Lutherans, and Baptists built Christian schools in Ramallah. By the late 1800s, the Quakers had opened several small schools for girls, as well as a medical facility, and by 1910 they established a house of worship—a Friends Meeting House—in the center of the city.

After the first and second world wars, most of the Christians in Ramallah emigrated to the United States in search opportunity and prosperity. As a result of this exodus, Muslims from the surrounding Arab towns quickly bought up the property of their former neighbors.

Today the city of Ramallah and the surrounding region is home to more than 600,000 Palestinians. Fatah—the political arm of the Palestinian National Authority founded by Yasser Arafat in 1959 and currently led by Mahmoud Abbas—governs the West Bank. Before Abbas assumed the role of prime minister in 2003, Yasser Arafat had enjoyed a long and inglorious reign as unchallenged terrorist leader of Fatah and the PLO, and in 1996, he became the first president of the Palestinian Authority.

Under Arafat's control for decades, Ramallah gained a dubious reputation for violence and turmoil. Rampant poverty added to the misery of the Palestinian people. Sadly, even after Arafat's death in 2004, the chaos continued unabated for several years. Religious and ethnic reprisals and the struggle for power between Islamic rivals Hamas and Hezbollah kept Ramallah's streets tense.

But in 2008, a fragile peace blossomed, and today a compassionate move of God is underway, breathing life and hope into this ravaged city and reigniting its ancient Christian heritage. Because of the faithfulness of young Palestinians like Rafi and Hanifah and the Ramallah Teahouse, Ramallah has become home to several small yet vibrant fellowships of Palestinian believers.

Rafi's heartfelt words still echo in my mind whenever I think about the Palestinian people: "Most of all, remember to pray for us!"

Ramallah – West Bank, Israel

Ramallah – West Bank, Israel

CHAPTER TWELVE

The Hunt for Osama

Khartoum, Sudan

A scorching hot sun was rising over Khartoum, the capitol city of Sudan, Africa's largest country. The intense sunlight penetrated the sand-laden Sahara air as it wafted through the narrow streets, creating a red Martian-like atmosphere in this sprawling desert metropolis on the Upper Nile. Droning calls to prayer resonated from hundreds of mosque minarets rising above mud-thatched rooftops, reminding Muslims of their unyielding loyalty to Allah.

The streets were filled with people in motion—ten million of them, all intent on reaching their destinations. Horns honked and bicycle bells clanged for attention. Little three-wheel motorcycle taxis puffed black exhaust fumes as they darted in and out of traffic, adding to the chaos and congestion. Dark-skinned men donning traditional white robes and turbans squatted near crude roadside stands, sipping cups of hot sweet tea.

A young Sudanese man walked with a steady gait past the mosque, undeterred by the call coming from the loudspeakers. He was answering a different call to prayer—at a local Christian church. That night, Osama would attend his first official Bible class in preparation for becoming a pastor.

Osama came from a Muslim village in northern Sudan, and his parents had raised him in strict adherence to Islamic *(sharia)* law. Every Friday without fail, Osama had attended prayers at the local mosque with his father. But as a teenager, Osama began to grow disinterested in religion and the Islamic faith. During a period of rebellion, he ran away from home, fleeing to the sprawling metropolis of Khartoum. It was there he discovered the Believer's Church and heard about Jesus Christ for the first time in his life.

In this church, filled with Sudanese believers from across the country, Osama learned that God loved him, created him for a divine purpose, and was reaching out to him. Osama was amazed that he could know this God in a personal way, not just through religious rituals.

Through the loving support of his new church family, Osama grew in his faith and began to sense a purpose for his life. He dedicated himself to fervently study the Bible so he could learn more about God and His Son, Jesus, and teach others about God's grace and love.

On my way to the Believer's Church, I thought about the invitation I had received months before from the pastor.

"Please come and teach our Sudanese students, brother!" he wrote. "They are hungry to learn more of God's Word."

Me teach? I thought as I read the words. *I'm not a teacher. My spiritual gifts are to exhort, encourage, and assist? I know many more qualified men who could go.*

But when I told a ministry colleague about the invitation, he advised me to accept it. With his prodding and encouragement, I finally agreed to go.

Over the years, I had heard quite a bit about the conflicts and ethnic "cleansings" that had plagued Sudan and had seen the suffering of the Sudanese people on television. But I had to confess that I didn't know very much about what God was doing in this war-torn country.

Glancing at my watch as I approached the church entrance, I realized that my first teaching session was just about to begin. My stomach, which had been relatively well behaved moments before, suddenly began doing flip-flops. In an effort to calm my nerves, I prayed that God would help me share His Word in a way the students could easily understand and that I wouldn't embarrass myself by bumbling through the lesson.

The building didn't resemble what most Westerners would think of as a church. The crude concrete blocks retained the heat of the day, and by the time I entered the tiny sanctuary, it felt like a sauna at 93 degrees Fahrenheit. A wobbly ceiling fan was the only consolation for those who had gathered to pray and study the Bible. The blades looked as if they would fly off the fan at any moment and decapitate someone.

The harsh glow of a lone fluorescent bulb illuminated the pale white ceiling and green walls, giving the room an other-world aura.

Joining us that hot, muggy evening in May were several young Sudanese men and women. There were also visitors from southern Sudan. Distinctly taller than their northern Sudanese brothers and sisters, their smooth, shiny black skin glistened like polished ebony, and their high cheekbones immediately set them apart from those of Arab descent. Also in attendance was a young refugee couple from Eritrea, a small region in northern Ethiopia embroiled in civil war.

As the room fill with students, I took a seat next to a young Sudanese man.

"Hello! My name is David," I said by way of introduction.

"My name is Osama," the young man said with a radiant white smile.

I raised my eyebrows in surprise at his name.

"Oh, don't be afraid," he said, laughing. "I am not related to the Osama you Americans are looking for. Osama is a very common name for boys here. Believe me, if I knew where bin Laden was, I would gladly turn him in for the reward. My family is very poor, and we could use the money!"

Other students joined in the lighthearted moment, and we all had a good laugh.

"You see, David," Osama continued, his expression turning serious, "I want to live in peace and have the freedom to worship the true God. I came from a very strict Muslim village in northern Sudan. When I fled my village, I had no one to care for me. Some of my friends accused me of disgracing my family and my faith. I came to Khartoum because I wanted freedom from religion and to live my life as I wanted to live it. Little did I realize that God was searching for me, seeking me out because He wanted to know me.

"Now I have found Jesus and others who also believe in him. We have similar backgrounds and stories, and we encourage each other and look out for one another. I have tried to go back to my hometown, but most of my relatives and neighbors don't want to hear the message of God's love.

"Here in Khartoum we meet secretly to talk about God and Jesus. We feel strongly that God is going to use us as pastors and missionaries to win many Muslims to Jesus Christ in the coming days. We pray daily for our Muslim neighbors and friends to come to know Him, but they need to hear God's Word. They are just like I was. How can they believe in Jesus unless they hear of Him? That is why we are here tonight—to be taught so we can go out and share God's Word! We need men like you and your friends from America to come and teach us!

"The Islamic leadership in Sudan proudly declares that our country is the gateway for an Islamic revolution in Africa. But we, the church of Jesus Christ, see Sudan as the gateway for the kingdom of God, spread the gospel to North Africa, Saudi Arabia, and the heart of the Muslim world in the Middle East!

"Brother David, do your Christian friends in America know there are believers in Sudan? I think they know about Darfur and our war, but do they know that there are young men like me—Osamas who are not terrorists? You see, brother David, America isn't the only kingdom looking for Osama. Our Father God is also looking for Osamas just like me to redeem as servants for His kingdom!"

With another huge grin on his face, Osama hugged me and said,

"Please let your people know that you have found Osama and that he is not a terrorist!"

For more than thirty years, one of the worst civil wars in the history of humankind raged in Sudan.[1] Carried out between Arab-influenced Muslims in the north and orthodox Christians in the south, the resurgence of racial and religious bloodshed between these two groups from 1983 through 2005—the Second Sudanese Civil War—was essentially the continuation of a bitter, centuries-old conflict.

According to a U.S. Committee on Refugees and Immigrants (USCRI) report in 1998, more than 1.9 million people died in Sudan between 1983 and 1998 as a result of the civil war, and more than 4 million people were internally displaced as a result of the fighting. In 2003, the suffering in Sudan reared its ugly head once again as the genocide in Darfur began. According to more recent estimates, the number of people killed by the Sudanese-sponsored Janjaweed militia—"devils on horseback," as they are called—topped 500,000, with nearly 2 million people displaced.

In the midst of this caldron of turmoil, a radical Islamic organization called al-Qaida—"the base"—took root in the 1990s. Their leader was Osama bin Laden, a citizen of Saudi Arabia and the son of a wealthy construction tycoon. Bin Laden and his followers quickly found favor with the Islamic leaders in Sudan's government and established strong business ties in the country and community.

By the late 1990s, Bin Laden had solidified his organization within Sudan and was using the country to mastermind terror attacks on U.S. interests in the region.

On August 7, 1998, a suicide truck bomb destroyed the U.S. embassy in Nairobi, Kenya, killing twelve Americans and two hundred Kenyans and injuring more than four thousand civilians. Simultaneously, a second truck bomb exploded outside the U.S. embassy in Dar es Salaam, Tanzania, killing twelve civilians and injuring eighty-five. Immediately the CIA pointed the finger at bin Laden as the mastermind of the attack, with support from other African nations; namely, Sudan.

On August 20, 1998, President Clinton ordered a cruise missile strike on a pharmaceutical factory on the outskirts of Khartoum, citing it as the primary supplier of the chemicals used in the bombs. Another U.S. strike targeted alleged terrorist training camps in Kandahar, Afghanistan, where it was believed that bin Laden and many of his leaders were meeting to discuss future attacks on U.S. interests around the world. Even though both targets were hit and destroyed, bin Laden survived and lived to plan the horrific attacks on the World Trade Center on September 11, 2001.

Nine years later, continued crisis and suffering have kept Sudan at the center of the world stage. As of 2009, an estimated 2.7 million people or more had been internally displaced as a result of the humanitarian disaster in Darfur, driven from their homes by violence and the threat of starvation. The most recent United Nations report set the death toll from Sudan's civil war at a conservative figure of 300,000.

On March 4, 2009, the International Criminal Court at the

Hague issued an arrest warrant for Sudan president Omar al-Bashir for war crimes and crimes against humanity. Defiantly, al-Bashir told reporters that the warrant wasn't "worth the ink" it was written in and then began dancing while supporters burned an image of the chief prosecutor in effigy.[2]

In spite of ongoing ethnic conflict, extreme hostility toward Christians, and strict enforcement of *sharia* law, I believe there is hope for Sudan. Since the bilateral peace agreement was signed in January of 2005, both northern and southern Sudan have experienced a fragile peace and relative stability. During this time, the church in southern Sudan has experienced tremendous growth, with many ministries from Kenya and neighboring regions launching evangelistic efforts to reach the Sudanese people. Recent estimates indicate that more than six million Christians live in southern Sudan.[3] In the north, where the population is mostly Sunni Muslim, the numbers of true believers has been more difficult to determine. But some estimate it at close to two million.

Included in these estimates are young believers like Osama, whom God is calling to serve Him as pastors and Bible teachers. Hope for Sudan is found in these courageous Sudanese Christians, several of whom I had the joy of teaching that night in a tiny church in Khartoum!

Sudan

سيرة
منافذ

ENTRY

EGYPT

CHAPTER THIRTEEN

Miracles on the Nile

Cairo, Egypt

Billows of black smoke belched from a rusty bulldozer parked outside a small brick building in the El Shahid district outside Cairo. The bulldozer operator waved his arms and shook his fist in the air. *"Allahu akbar! Allahu akbar!* Death to the Christians!" he shouted.

Inside the tiny building, a Christian pastor huddled together with several other believers as they prayed for God to intervene on their behalf. The growl of the diesel engine loudly declared the evil intentions of the Muslim workers who had assembled outside. Pastor Abdullah rose and walked over to the window. He couldn't believe his eyes. The bulldozer operator was determined to raze the church to the ground in the name of Allah.

The pastor had received an ominous warning several days earlier from Abbas, an official at the Ministry of Religion. "You are violating Islamic law!" Abbas had threatened. "If you continue to hold meetings and teach people about Jesus and the Bible, I will force you to close your doors!"

The believers had been concerned about what the government official might do, but no one thought he would resort to this. They had underestimated the seriousness of his threat and were surprised when the bulldozer roared to life outside the church as Pastor Abdullah and his congregation worshiped inside.

As the conflict escalated, Pastor Abdullah led the small group of believers in songs of praise to God. Men, women, and children cried out in prayer, asking God to spare their lives and the church they had labored so hard to build. Sensing that Abbas might abandon his evil plans if the church was filled with people, Pastor Abdullah instructed several members of his congregation to call other believers on their cell phones, asking them to bring supplies and join in the vigil. Within thirty minutes, more than fifty people arrived at the church and squeezed into the tiny sanctuary for a Christian-style sit-in.

Lifting his voice in prayer, Pastor Abdullah declared his trust in God: "Oh, Lord, You are the only God, the God over Egypt and the world! You have brought Your children here to be Your hands of love to the people of El Shahid. Now Pharaoh and his army have come! Our backs are against the Red Sea, and we cannot go forward without Your help. Just as You helped Moses and the children of Israel, please hear us and deliver us this day!"

When Abbas heard what was happening at the church, he

returned later that afternoon only to find the believers praising God. He had expected his threats to strike such fear in their hearts that they would quickly comply with his demands. But they seemed more determined than ever to continue worshiping their God.

Angered by their resistance, Abbas once again threatened Pastor Abdullah. "I have ordered the dozer operator to go home. If you and your people agree to stop meeting together and leave the building immediately, we will take the bulldozer away in the morning and won't bother you anymore. But if I find you here tomorrow, I will destroy this building and any who remain inside!"

As night fell on El Shahid, Pastor Abdullah and the believers decided to continue their prayer vigil. There was no doubt in their minds that if they left the church, Abbas would return with the bulldozer operator during the night and tear down the building.

Friends brought food and other supplies from the market, as well as small straw mattresses for people to sleep on. The group huddled around small kerosene lamps as they ate their meager dinner. Then Pastor Abdullah divided them into smaller groups to keep watch through the long, dark night, lifting prayers for deliverance from those who wanted to destroy their church. While some of the believers slept, others prayed and sang praises to God, just as Paul and Silas had done long ago during their imprisonment in Macedonia.[1]

When the bright desert sun rose the next morning, word of Abbas's threat and the church's sit-in had already spread throughout the community. A crowd of curious onlookers gathered across from the church to see what would happen. Standing nearby, an elder from the local mosque in a long white robe observed the scene in silence, his face wrinkled from the harsh Sahara winds. Children played in the trash-strewn water canals along the streets as young girls with brass water pots balanced on their heads mingled shyly among the crowd, listening to the prayers and singing coming from the church. Burros pulling wooden carts piled high with lush green grass from the banks of the Nile plodded slowly down the narrow dirt streets.

"They have been singing all night," a woman in the crowd whispered.

"I haven't seen this kind of faith since my childhood," mumbled an old man.

At nine o'clock, Abbas returned to the church, but the angry bulldozer operator wasn't with him. In hushed anticipation, the crowd watched the government official walk down the street and march right up to the church entrance.

"Open the door, Abdullah!" Abbas shouted, pounding on the door.

Pastor Abdullah slowly opened the door, breathing a silent prayer for God's protection.

"I hear that you and your people spent the entire night praying and worshiping your God. Is this true?" Abbas demanded.

"Yes, this is true," Pastor Abdullah replied in a humble voice, noticing the puzzled expression on the official's face.

Abbas glanced at the crowd assembled across the street and then returned his gaze to Pastor Abdullah. With a set jaw, the official said, "Even though you violated my orders, I have decided not to prosecute you or destroy this building. As a Muslim, I pray five times a day and worship at the mosque every Friday, but I have never seen such dedication to God as you and your people have shown.

Who am I to fight against you and Him? You are free to continue worshiping your God as you please. I will not bother you anymore."

As Abbas turned to walk away, Abdullah called out, emboldened by the miracle he had just witnessed. "Sir, you can also know this God we pray to. *Inshallah* [God willing], we will continue meeting here to pray and worship God. You are always welcome to join us."

When the believers inside the church heard the conversation between Abbas and Pastor Abdullah, they erupted into songs of praise, thanking God for His deliverance. Their church and their lives had been spared because they had placed their trust in Him.

News of God's miraculous intervention spread like wildfire throughout El Shahid, and those gathered in the streets that morning marveled to see the bold and radiant faith of this committed group of Christians.

Today, the believers in El Shahid continue to meet together to worship God and grow in their faith and devotion to Christ. The prayer vigil they held that night at the church made a lasting impression upon Abbas and the Muslim community. Some have even expressed an interest in learning about this God who inspired such passionate devotion among His followers and delivered them from harm in such a powerful way.

Born and raised in an Orthodox Christian home, Adara attended Pastor Abdullah's church in El Shahid, Egypt, with her family for several years. Even though Adara grew up in a Christian environment, her relationship with God didn't become real to her until a traumatic experience that changed her life forever.

As a high-school student, Adara often interacted with Muslim girls at school. Subtly influenced by her friend Mika, Adara began to question the Bible and consider the claims of the Koran. One Friday, she went with Mika to pray at the local mosque, but when she arrived, Muslim officials abducted her and took her to the local police station. The officials filed false charges against her and told her that if she didn't convert to Islam and marry her friend's brother, she would be tried and convicted for speaking blasphemies against the Koran. The local imam even brought documents to the jail and demanded that she sign them, formally declaring her conversion from Christianity to Islam and clearing the way for her to marry. But in spite of extreme duress, Adara refused to sign the papers.

As soon as Pastor Abdullah heard of her abduction, he rushed to the police station to intervene on her behalf. When he entered the jail cell, he was horrified to find Adara under the influence of a very strong drug. He pleaded with the authorities for her release, but to no avail. Pastor Abdullah prayed with Adara before leaving the jail and assured her that he would do everything possible to secure her release. Then he called on his tiny congregation to fast and pray around the clock for God to deliver Adara from her Muslim captors.

After spending several days in jail, Adara was taken to an apartment near the home of the young man she was being forced to marry. Unknown to her abductors, her family's apartment was just across the street. One morning while looking out the living-room window, Adara saw her older brother, Ghassan. Grabbing a plate from the kitchen, she hurled it through the window and frantically called out to Ghassan until he looked up and recognized her.

When her brother broke into the apartment to rescue Adara, she ran into his arms sobbing. She had never been so happy to see him in her life. Ghassan tried to comfort his distraught sister, promising to take her to Pastor Abdullah's home, where he believed she would be safe.

Quickly escaping down the stairwell of the apartment building, Ghassan and Adara melted into the crowded marketplaces of El Shahid. To ensure they weren't being followed, Ghassan led his sister through a maze of side streets to the pastor's apartment. As Ghassan rapped persistently on the door, Adara prayed they wouldn't draw attention. Pastor Abdullah's house was always being monitored by Muslim extremists, and if they discovered that she was hiding there, they would surely take her back to the police station and punish Pastor Abdullah.

Finally the door opened slightly, and the pastor's wife, Jameela, peered out at them. Seeing Adara's tear-stained face, she threw the door open wide and drew the young woman into a motherly embrace. "It's a miracle!" Jameela exclaimed. "God has answered our prayers!"

Pastor Abdullah quickly ushered everyone inside so they wouldn't be seen by religious police who might be watching the house.

While Jameela prepared cups of hot tea for Adara and her brother, Adara poured out her harrowing tale of captivity. Adara confessed to Pastor Abdullah how wrong she had been to doubt her faith in Christ and how close she had come to being forced to convert to Islam. "I know I was influenced by my friends at school. I was lonely at home and thought no one cared about me or my needs. I believed that I would find companionship in Islam, but everything my friend told me was a lie. While I was imprisoned in jail, I wondered whether God had abandoned me, but I kept praying and refused to give in to the authorities' demands. God answered my prayers for deliverance!

Now I know that He is real and that He loves me!"

The pastor replied with a gentle smile, "We all question our faith at times, but the Lord is faithful to bring us back to the truth. Sometimes He allows us to experience what life would be like without Him so that we will be truly thankful for all He has given us in Christ. God never left you, Adara, even though you left Him for a time. He brought you safely back to us!"

Pastor Abdullah and his family hid Adara in their home for several weeks, until the police dropped their charges and the local imam gave up his attempt to convert her to Islam. At Pastor Abdullah's home, Adara found the comfort and shelter she needed to recover from the trauma she had experienced, and soon she rededicated her life to Christ.

Today, Adara is married to a faithful Christian man from Pastor Abdullah's church and recently gave birth to their first child. Adara's story is another powerful reminder that God protects those who belong to Him and often intervenes in miraculous ways in the most desperate situations.

God has been performing miracles in Egypt for millennia, but throughout the history of this ancient land, nothing has surpassed the miracles He performed when He brought His people out of Egypt, delivering them from more than four hundred years of bondage. (See Exodus 7–12.)

Most of us could recite the age-old story of the Exodus from memory, but not many Christians in the West understand the spiritual significance of the ten plagues God sent to afflict Pharaoh and his people. In a display of matchless power, God challenged the gods of Egypt, cursing the very essence of their existence. As He unleashed each plague upon the Egyptians, one by one, the gods they trusted in for protection fell in defeat before the living God. First, God moved His hand over the Nile River, the domain of Khnum, the Giver of the Nile, and the waters turned to blood.[2] Pharaoh pleaded with Moses to ask his God to remove this scourge, but when the waters were restored to health, Pharaoh hardened his heart, refusing to set the Israelites free.

Time and again, God showed Pharaoh that all of nature belonged to Him. Frogs, lice, flies, and locusts swarmed over the land, but the gods of Egypt were powerless to stop them. Yet Pharaoh's heart remained hardened. Disease and sickness afflicted livestock and people alike, but when the Egyptians cried out to Isis, the goddess of life and healing, the heavens were silent. When God moved his hand again, darkness came over the land, blocking out the rays of the sun god Ra. The God of heaven seemed to laugh as He exposed the gods of Egypt for what they really were.

But suddenly the laughter stopped, and the final plague fell upon the firstborn males of Egypt. From the least to the greatest, from slaves to Pharaoh's son, death struck a crushing blow. No one in all of Egypt was spared—except God's people. When the angel of death saw the blood on the doorposts of Israelite homes, he stayed his hand. The children of Israel were not to be touched because the almighty God was their protection.

Broken at last by the heavy hand of God, Pharaoh relented and let the Israelites go. But shortly afterward, he had second thoughts and, with his army, pursued the Israelites to the edge of the Red Sea, threatening to slaughter thousands of men, women, and children. But the living God heard the cries of His people and opened up a path through the sea until all of them passed safely across to the other side. The Egyptian army pursued the Israelites, but once again God moved His hand, and the waters swallowed up the soldiers and their horses.

The power of Egypt was no match for the living God!

Regarded by many as the cradle of human civilization, ancient Egypt was renowned for its engineering feats, such as the great pyramids of Giza, and its powerful pharaohs, adorned in elaborate robes and headdresses. The land of Egypt, with its timeless Nile River and its dizzying array of gods, has enchanted tourists for millennia. In modern times, Egypt has become the bastion of Islamic academia. The al-Azhar University in Cairo, one of the world's oldest institutions, and the al-Azhar Mosque are revered by Muslims around the world.

Although modern-day Egypt has lost much of its ancient glory, it remains a land of mystery—and miracles. But there are dark corners in Egypt that most tourists never see. Impoverished areas like El Shahid. A sprawling district on the outskirts of Cairo, El Shahid is one of the poorest slums along the Nile River. With a population of more than one hundred thousand Muslims, the city is predominately controlled by radical Islamic clerics.

When Pastor Abdullah and his family moved to El Shahid eight years ago, there was no Christian presence in the city. Friends and relatives questioned his decision, but Pastor Abdullah believed that

God was calling his family to this spiritually dark community to preach the gospel and serve the poor. Abdullah, his wife, Jameela, and their two young children gave up a comfortable life and a successful ministry at a well-known Christian church in downtown Cairo to reach out to the Muslims of El Shahid, using a small vacant storefront shop as a church. In the early days, the family lived in a tiny apartment, and Pastor Abdullah made just enough money from odd jobs to pay the rent and buy a little food to sustain his family.

On the first Sunday Pastor Abdullah opened the church doors, his congregation consisted of just his wife and children. Yet God remained faithful. Nestled among the Muslim population of El Shahid, the church slowly began to grow, and soon more than fifty members squeezed into the small storefront facility. Many church members came from the Upper Nile regions of Egypt and were extremely poor. More than 65 percent of the congregation was illiterate, and some were widows, whose husbands had been killed by radical Islamic militants. In spite of their poverty, Pastor Abdullah asked the members to contribute whatever they could and trust God to multiply their offerings so they could build a larger place of worship.

In a spirit of humble obedience, the congregation of El Shahid responded with overwhelming generosity. Some gave small amounts of money; others offered their gold and silver jewelry, and a young bride and groom gave their wedding rings. One lady brought two duck eggs, much like the widow Jesus honored in Luke 21, who gave all she had to live on. With the sacrificial gifts of the tiny congregation and support from a few churches in America, Pastor Abdullah was able to purchase a small piece of land and begin construction on a new meeting place.

Today, construction continues on the little church. The first and second floors have been completed, and a small balcony on the second floor has created additional space for worshipers. In the fall of 2008, workers built concrete columns to support a third floor, but angry Muslims tore them down a few months later during the Islamic holy day of *Eid al Adha*.

In spite of severe trials and persecution, Pastor Abdullah and the fellowship in El Shahid continue to share their faith in Issa with their Muslim neighbors. And although the believers themselves struggle to make ends meet, they lovingly feed the poor and care for orphans in their community. Every Sunday the church meets to worship God and study His Word, and on Fridays, the women operate a special Bible ministry for children. Ironically, many wealthy Muslim women enroll their children in this Bible program so they can socialize at the local mosque during Friday prayers.

There are still poor families in the fellowship at El Shahid, but Pastor Abdullah and his congregation are seeking to create new opportunities for employment. Several sewing machines have been purchased so that ladies in the church can make bed sheets and pillow cases to sell in the marketplace. The church also plans to start a small medical clinic in the community to offer care to the poor.

Pastor Abdullah's vibrant congregation stands as a powerful testimony of His protection and deliverance as they shine the light of His grace and love on the Muslim community in El Shahid. God is still performing miracles on the Nile!

Egypt

Egypt

CHAPTER FOURTEEN

Pastor Tom's Change of Heart

United States of America

In 2001, my friend Tom was the senior pastor of a large church in Cerritos, California. A soft-spoken, teddy bear of a man, Tom had a heart for people and was well liked by everyone he met. His Mexican ancestry also gave him a unique understanding and appreciation of the ethnic diversity of Southern California.

As a pastor, Tom preached God's grace and love for all people, but when Islamic terrorists attacked the World Trade Center on September 11, 2001, the seeds of prejudice that had lurked undetected in his heart sprang to life and began to spread their deadly tentacles.

Like many Americans, Tom reacted in shock and outrage as he watched the World Trade Center towers collapse again and again in nonstop media coverage. Weeping bitter tears over such a devastating loss of life, he wondered how God could have allowed terrorists to kill so many innocent people in the name of Allah. Tom had witnessed firsthand the death and destruction Islamic militants inflicted on the people of southern Sudan when he visited the country in the late 1990s, but now terrorists were attacking his homeland. He couldn't believe his eyes.

The morning after the attacks, Tom placed six large American flags in his front yard in a show of solidarity with his fellow Americans and a tribute to those who had been killed in the name of jihad. As the days passed, he struggled with an overwhelming range of feelings, from heartbreak and grief to confusion, fear, and anger. Even though he preached God's forgiveness and grace, Tom was filled with hatred for these terrorists from Saudi Arabia. They deserved judgment, not mercy! Blood for blood, these murderers had to pay with their lives!

When I spoke with Tom shortly after the attacks, I was stunned at the bitterness that poured out of him. I could understand his anger over what had happened and his desire for justice, but I was deeply disturbed by his contempt toward anyone of Middle Eastern descent—Muslim or not. I couldn't believe that a Christian— especially a pastor—would want to condemn the Muslim people to an eternity separated from the God who loved them and sent His Son to die for them.

Tom seemed unaware of his prejudice toward Muslims, and with each passing year, his heart became more callous. Whenever he heard about some tragedy in the Middle East, instead of feeling profound empathy for the people, he secretly rejoiced. These people deserved God's wrath!

Blind to his prejudice and hard-heartedness, Tom continued to lead his congregation as if nothing had changed. He preached about God's love and His offer of salvation to everyone, just as he had always done. He also organized missions trips to help hurting people in places like southern Sudan and Sri Lanka, where Muslims were persecuting Christians.

Then one day in 2008, in a twist of godly irony, Tom was invited to join several other senior pastors on a missions trip to Iraq to train indigenous pastors. Like the prophet Jonah in the Old Testament, Tom began to question God. *Why would you send me to Iraq? They're the enemy...cold-blooded killers! How can you ask me to love people who not only hate America but hate You and Your people?*

Tom wrestled over the decision for weeks, but in the end, he took a gigantic leap of faith and accepted the invitation. He knew that God was calling him outside his comfort zone and that he was about to be stretched in ways he couldn't possibly imagine.

In September, as Tom reluctantly boarded an airplane bound for Amman, Jordan, he thought back seven years to the events of 9/11. Time had smoothed the sharp edges off the rage and grief he once felt, but he knew he would never forget what Middle Eastern terrorists had done in the name of Allah.

When Tom arrived in Jordan, he was carrying more than travel baggage; he was lugging around a heavy load of bitterness, suspicion, and prejudice toward the Middle Eastern people that had formed a thick shell around his heart. But during the layover in Jordan, God performed a heart transplant on Tom.

Since Tom and his colleagues would be spending several hours in Amman before departing for Iraq, they decided to walk to a nearby shopping mall to get a cup of coffee. Looking at all the people on the busy streets, Tom began to realize that they weren't much different from him. He watched men and women strolling along with their children, laughing and eating ice cream. At the mall, he saw young Jordanians wearing Western jeans and T-shirts, just like young people in Southern California.

Then, to his amazement, Tom spotted a Starbucks coffee shop! Entering the shop, he was surprised to see men and women laughing and having animated conversations while they enjoyed their coffee. It seemed as if he was back in Southern California—but this was Jordan! Weren't these people Muslims, America's enemies?

As Tom walked back to the guesthouse, he thought about the Middle Eastern people he had seen that day and realized that they were created in God's image, just like him. Jesus had died for their sins and offered them salvation too. Did God love him more than any of these people? Suddenly Tom became painfully aware of his own self-righteousness, spiritual pride, and prejudice. He felt deeply ashamed. How could he harbor bitterness in his heart against these people any longer? At that moment, God began to melt Tom's racist heart.

Arriving back at the guesthouse, Tom shared his life-changing experience with some of the team members as tears of remorse streamed down his face. As he told me later, "In an instant, God touched me and gave me a new heart. He replaced my hatred and bitterness toward the Middle Eastern people. For the first time in my life, I saw them through God's eyes. As I wept in shame and repentance, God burned into me a love not only for the Jordanian people but for all the people of the Middle East. I felt like the Grinch on Mount Crumpit. I had a brand new heart!"

When Tom arrived in Iraq the next day, God gave him so much love and compassion for the Iraqi people that he decided to return in 2009 to continue preparing Iraqi pastors for the ministry. As of this writing, Tom is considering moving his entire family to this part of the world, where he hopes to work alongside Iraqi churches in a teaching capacity.

Tom's story is all too common in a post-9/11 world. Most Americans can identify with what Tom felt after the terrorist attacks, and many even harbor prejudice against people from the Middle East—especially Muslims. Sadly, like Pastor Tom, even those of us who are Christians have allowed the seeds of hatred to grow in our hearts toward Muslims. Just because we belong to the Lord doesn't mean we're immune from prejudice!

Immediately following the attacks on the World Trade Center, a pastor told me, "The only way to rid the world of terrorism is to drop a nuclear bomb on the Muslims!"

I was stunned. His bitter, self-righteous response reminded me of the way Jesus' disciples reacted toward the Samaritans who refused to allow Jesus into their village. An outraged James and John asked

Jesus, "Lord, do you want us to call fire down from heaven to destroy them?" (Luke 9:54).

To the disciples, who believed their Jewish heritage was superior to every other ethnic group, the Samaritans were defiled and worthless. Not only were they inferior culturally and spiritually; they were illegitimate children, religious bastards worthy of condemnation because they didn't worship the true God. People like this deserved God's wrath, not His mercy. And yet Jesus rebuked His disciples for their racist attitudes (verse 55).

Even the prophet Jonah harbored prejudice in his heart. God commanded him to go to Nineveh (the modern-day city of Mosul in northern Iraq) and preach the way of salvation to the people who lived there. God planned to destroy the Ninevites because of their wickedness, but He wanted to give them one more chance to repent and escape His wrath. But Jonah didn't think the Ninevites deserved God's mercy. In Jonah's prejudiced mind, the people of Nineveh were incapable of repentance and rightfully deserved God's wrath for the atrocities they had committed against the Jews.

Jonah couldn't have cared less about the Ninevites, but they were important to God! Prejudice had blinded Jonah to God's heart for these lost people, so to open the prophet's eyes, God allowed a giant fish to swallow him. After sloshing around in the fish's belly for a few days, Jonah repented of his spiritual pride and vowed to carry out God's assignment.

Soon after Jonah lifted his humble prayer of repentance to God, the fish deposited Jonah on a sandy piece of shoreline near the metropolitan city. Jonah brushed himself off and made his way into

Nineveh, wandering through the streets and marketplaces preaching repentance.

The Ninevites listened to Jonah and turned from their wickedness. But the prophet was furious! In a tirade, he complained to God, "I knew you wouldn't destroy these people! You are too compassionate and merciful for that. You have spared their lives, but now take mine. I would be better off dead!"

The roots of prejudice ran deep in Jonah's stony heart, and it would take more surgery to complete the transformation God was bringing about. But that day in a pagan city, Jonah caught a small glimpse of God's love for the Ninevites, no matter how wicked or undeserving they were. Jonah began to understand that God's plan of salvation included all people, regardless of their ethnic background or religious beliefs.

Just as Jonah and Jesus' disciples justified their own prejudice, Pastor Tom once believed that his hatred of Muslims was justified. Sadly, many Christians in America today would agree. After all, they reason, the terrorists who killed thousands of innocent people on 9/11 were Muslims, and all Muslims hate Americans and want to destroy our way of life! Even worse, they despise peace-loving Christians around the world, calling us infidels and dedicating themselves to a holy war against us. In their hostility against Christianity, Muslims forfeit the grace and love God offers through His Son, Jesus. They deserve God's wrath!

Many of us may view the Islamic world this way, but is this how God sees Muslims? Does He rejoice when the tyrants of this world—including Saddam Hussein and the 9/11 terrorists—receive the death sentences they deserve? Or does He grieve over the souls of men who have been condemned to eternal separation from Him?

As radical as it sounds, the Bible says that God doesn't want "anyone to perish, but *everyone* to come to repentance" (2 Peter 3:9, emphasis added). Jesus died for all people (2 Corinthians 5:14-15), and His love extends even to the Middle East! He even loves suicide jihadists whose hearts are filled with so much hatred for the West that they willingly fly passenger airplanes into skyscrapers!

Most Christians talk about the love of Christ, but when it comes to the Muslim world, do our actions match our words? Or have we allowed our hearts to become hardened by bitterness and prejudice? Like Pastor Tom, are we unaware of the more subtle forms of prejudice that may be lurking undetected within our hearts? Do we justify ourselves by hiding behind a cloak of self-righteous indignation?

The story of Saul in the book of Acts is a powerful illustration of God's ability to transform hearts that have been hardened by prejudice and spiritual pride. A Jew by birth, Saul was a very devout, self-righteous man who had received the best religious training at the feet of Rabbi Gamaliel. Saul was a Pharisee of the Pharisees, a man of religious and nationalistic fervor, perfect in every way when it came to keeping God's law and following the traditions of Judaism. Saul's passion for God and his Jewish faith were unmatched. He loved those who loved God and hated those who hated Him. He truly thought he was a defender and protector of God's truth—a truth he was willing to die for. The only problem was that Saul's religious zeal was deeply misguided.

Starting with his complicity in the murder of Stephen, a Christ-follower, Saul began a terror campaign against Christians in the Holy Land. He pursued believers from town to town, had them imprisoned, and sought their execution (Acts 7:54–8:3). Then one day on a hate-filled mission to persecute believers in Syria, Saul came face-to-face with Jesus (Acts 9:1-5).

In a supernatural encounter with the risen Lord, Saul was blinded by a brilliant light from heaven and fell to the ground like a dead man.

A voice thundered all around him, "Saul, why are you persecuting Me?"

"Who are you?" Saul stammered.

"I am Jesus, the One you are persecuting!" the voice echoed.

Stumbling to his feet, Saul groped around in darkness, his sight taken from him.

Saul's men led him by the hand into Damascus, where he found lodging at the house of a man named Judas. For three days, Saul sat in total darkness, overwhelmed and confused by what had happened to him. His companions encouraged him to eat, but he refused.

Then a follower of Jesus named Ananias arrived to speak with Saul. Laying hands on the blind zealot, Ananias said, "Brother Saul, the Lord—Jesus, who appeared to you on the road as you were coming here—has sent me so that you may see again and be filled with the Holy Spirit" (Acts 9:17).

At that moment, Saul's sight was restored, and he began to see the world anew through God's eyes. A man whose name was feared by Christians throughout Palestine received a new name—Paul—and devoted his life to preaching the gospel. If God changed the heart of a religious, ignorant zealot like Saul, He is able to change any heart, no matter how hard.

As Saul and Pastor Tom discovered, changing hearts is God's specialty! Only He can open our eyes to prejudice and spiritual pride and fill us with His love for people of all races, cultures, and religions—even Islamic terrorists!

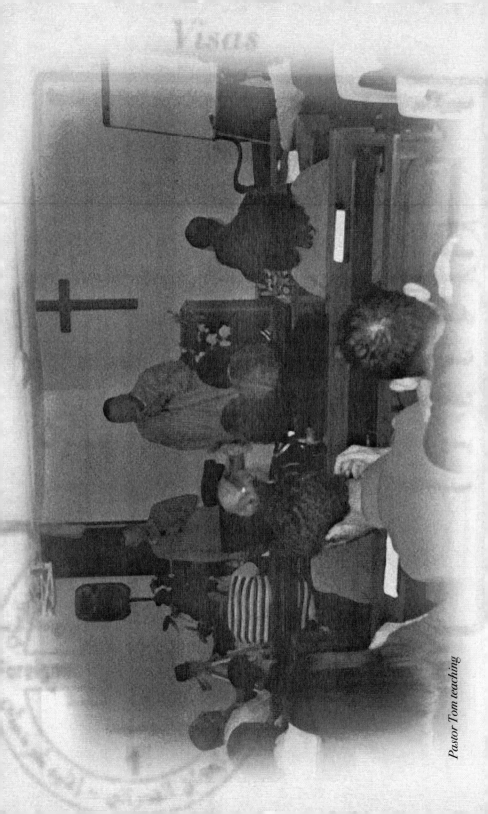

Pastor Tom teaching

CHAPTER FIFTEEN

A Modern-Day Pentecost

Kurdistan, Iraq-Iran Border

In September of 2008, I had the privilege of joining more than 650 pastors, Christian leaders, and other believers for a prayer conference in a remote region of Kurdistan along the Iraq-Iran border. We had come to worship God and lift our voices in prayer for our homelands. Many came from countries ravaged by war, poverty, and religious oppression. Some traveled by bus, car, or airplane; others arrived on foot. Some hailed from ancient cities in northern Iraq—Mosul (Nineveh in the Old Testament), Dohuk, Kirkuk, Erbil, Sulymania—and cities in the south, including Basra, Najaf, and Baghdad. Others came from Cairo, Egypt; Beirut, Lebanon; Istanbul, Turkey; and northwestern Iran. Crossing even greater distances were believers from Australia, the United Kingdom, New Zealand, Switzerland, Uganda, Canada, and the United States.

As the conference attendees packed into a simple meeting hall on a barren, rock-strewn hillside, I was amazed to see people from so many different countries and ethnic backgrounds. To outsiders, the gathering would have looked more like an OPEC meeting than a worship service. The air tingled with anticipation, and the hum of voices filled the hall as believers fellowshipped with one another.

Soon the worshipers erupted into exuberant songs of thanksgiving and praise to the Lord, lifting their voices in Arabic as the worship team led them. The melodious blend of voices and instruments rang throughout the hall as many of the young believers leaped and danced with joy while others waved colorful banners. It was a heavenly experience.

Each day of the conference, we heard story after story of those who had come to faith in Christ through visions and dreams or by reading an Arabic Bible they had been given. Several converts were baptized in a public confession of their faith.

Many from Middle Eastern countries had risked their lives for the opportunity to worship with other believers in this unlikely place. They shared powerful, faith-filled stories of how God had kept them safe in war zones, delivered them from the perils of kidnapping, and sustained them in the midst of religious persecution and ethnic harassment.

I was humbled by the incredible courage of these brothers and sisters in Christ. My own decision to make the trip had been filled with excitement and anticipation, not fear for my life. Apart from the usual inconveniences and weariness of traveling such a distance, I had suffered no hardships, perils, or persecution.

I was especially moved as I spoke with Ibrahim and his wife, Farah, former Shiite Muslims from Basra, Iraq, who risked everything to follow Christ.

"My wife and I came from radical Muslim families," Ibrahim told me. "After the war began in 2003, we desperately needed to know the true God. We heard about Issa from other Christians in Baghdad and gave our hearts to Him. When we told our families that we had become followers of Christ, they denounced us as dead. Even so, we discovered a new family among the believers at our church in Baghdad, and we dedicated ourselves to be part of the leadership there. We truly felt God was calling us to be pastors to start new churches throughout Iraq.

"We were excited about attending the prayer conference so that we could learn more about God. We knew we would face many dangers if we came, but we were determined to make the journey. Our trials began the moment we left Baghdad with a group from our church. As we headed north, our van was stopped at a Kurdish military checkpoint, and I presented our travel documents to the soldier on duty. Flipping through our identification papers, he suddenly became upset and ordered my wife and me out of the van at gunpoint.

"'You are Shia Muslims from Basra! Why are you traveling with these Chaldean Christians in Kurdistan?' he demanded in a harsh tone.

"'We are in Kurdistan to join with our Christian friends to learn more about Issa,' I responded.

"'That is impossible!' the soldier scoffed. 'You are a Muslim and a terrorist! Your passport and ID card say that you and your wife are Shia from Basra. Everyone knows that cesspool breeds terrorists. You are an enemy of the Kurds!'

"I smiled kindly at the man and said, 'It is true that my family is Shia and that we are from Basra, but my wife and I are Christians, followers of Issa. The people we are traveling with can tell you that we are Christians. We attend church with them in Baghdad; they know us. I study the Bible, not the Koran. Here, look at the pages in my Bible, and you will see where I have been reading.'

"Reaching into my backpack, I pulled out my Arabic Bible. The guard stiffened as I handed him it to him. He opened it cautiously and then turned it upside down and shook it violently. As he fanned the pages like a feather, a small photo slipped from the pages and fluttered to the ground. Bending down slowly, the soldier picked up the photo and examined it. Suddenly his eyes widened in shock and anger. 'They are terrorists, they are terrorists!' he shouted, leveling his automatic weapon at us.

"Several other soldiers grabbed our arms and pulled us into the guardhouse for further interrogation. Shaken, I silently breathed a prayer to the Lord. How could I have forgotten? The photo was a portrait of me dressed in black, holding a rocket launcher and posing in front of the martyr's creed as a warrior in the Shia militia of Basra. I carried this photo in my Bible to show people that God had mercy on me and rescued me from the grip of radical Islam.

"As my wife and I sat in the guardhouse, a wave of fear enveloped us. Farah buried her head in her hands and cried out to the Lord. I placed my arm around her shoulders and tried to comfort her as I raised my voice in prayer. 'God, You have called me like Abraham to leave my home and follow You. Now I am among the Kurds, who do not trust my people. They do not believe that I am a Christian. Please give me Your strength and boldness to share Your heart with these men. I was willing to become a martyr for Islam; now I am ready to be a martyr for Jesus! Make me shine like Your servant Stephen when he was stoned for his testimony about You.'

"As this prayer left my lips, a large Kurdish man wearing a black leather jacket entered the room. He slowly drew a pistol from his holster and laid it on the table directly in front of us. Lighting a cigarette, he blew the smoke upward toward the glaring lightbulb dangling from the ceiling. Silence filled the room.

"He examined our identification papers for several minutes and then fixed his cold, dark eyes on us before speaking. 'My name is Hassan, and I am from the Kurdish Intelligence Office. You claim you are Christians, but a Shia does not turn his back on his own religion. If your people knew of this, they would behead you,' he stated matter-of-factly.

"Taking a deep breath, I prayed for boldness as I responded, 'My wife and I were both devoted to Islam at one time. I followed the *mullahs* and the teachings of the Koran as a faithful Muslim. But the true Allah, the living God, had mercy on me and revealed Himself to me through His Son, Issa. At that moment I realized that I needed a Savior and asked God to forgive all my sins. Now I am a follower of Issa, the true Prophet of God, who died on a cross for me. I pray that all Iraqis—Shia, Sunni, Kurds, and Arabs—will come to know His love and grace.'

"As I spoke, I felt the presence of God's Spirit fill the room. Peace washed over me, and when I glanced over at my wife, I could tell that she felt it too.

"Hassan looked deep into my eyes and then studied the photo on the table in front of him. Then his eyes met mine once again. 'Ibrahim,' he said. 'I can see that you are no terrorist. You are not the same man in this picture. I believe you are who you say you are. You and your wife are free to go back to your people. Tell them about your faith in Issa. Perhaps they will come to know the true Allah—and maybe even we Kurds will come to know Him through you as well.'

"When my wife and I were reunited with our friends in the van, we all rejoiced as I told them about the boldness God gave me to share my faith in Issa with the Kurdish intelligence officer. It was a miracle!

"Now I understand why I was born into a strict Muslim family and why I studied in the *madrasah*. God let me learn everything the Muslims teach, so He can use me to lead them to Him. I am ready to go back and tell them about Issa. I am willing to die for my faith. I have already decided to be like Jesus. He was a martyr too!"

A growing number of Muslims like Ibrahim and Farah are coming to Christ in the twenty-first century. The life-giving waters Jesus promised to all who believe in Him are flooding the barren spiritual landscape of the Islamic world, washing away the heavy burdens of war, turmoil, and oppression that these desolate people have endured for centuries. The people of the Middle East are experiencing a newfound freedom in Christ never before seen in modern history.

Isaac's descendants—the Jewish people—aren't the only ones returning to the Promised Land and coming to faith in their Messiah, Yeshua. God is working among Ishmael's descendants as well, fulfilling His promise to make them into a great nation (Genesis 17:20). He is also moving in their hearts as they walk in the faith of their father Abraham, seeking to know the true God and His Son, Issa.

A modern-day Pentecost is taking place in the Middle East today! To understand this move of God's Spirit, we need to take a closer look at the historical roots of this event.

According to Leviticus 23:15-16, God established Pentecost as an everlasting ordinance for His people. The Feast of Pentecost, also known as the Feast of Weeks, was one of three festivals celebrated in Jerusalem each year. (The Feast of Unleavened Bread and the Feast of Tabernacles were the other festivals.) Three times a year, all of the male descendants of Israel (Jacob) were required to make their pilgrimage to the temple with their families. Pentecost was a time for the Jewish people to give thanks to God, offering sacrifices of grain gleaned from the summer wheat harvest in Israel.

The events recorded in Acts 2, which took place in Jerusalem during Pentecost in AD 33, transformed the spiritual landscape of the Middle East forever. Just fifty days after the death and resurrection of Jesus, Jerusalem was overflowing with pilgrims from every nation in the known world, all coming to offer their gifts to Jehovah. In the midst of this feast of harvest, God unveiled His master plan to gather people from every nation, people group, and language into

His kingdom. But as amazing as this event would be, it was only a foreshadowing of the heavenly scene the apostle John described in Revelation 7:

After this I looked and there before me was a great multitude that no one could count, from every nation, tribe, people and language, standing before the throne and in front of the Lamb. They were wearing white robes…and they cried out in a loud voice: "Salvation belongs to our God, who sits on the throne, and to the Lamb." (verses 9-10)

That day in Jerusalem, more than one hundred followers of Christ were gathered in an upper room, when a mighty rushing wind filled the entire house. As God poured out His Spirit on the disciples in a show of His power, tongues of fire flickered over each of them, and they began praising God in languages from every corner of the globe.

Filled with the Spirit and overwhelmed with joy, the disciples staggered out onto the streets below. Hearing them "declaring the wonders of God" in so many diverse languages (Acts 2:11), those who had come to Jerusalem from distant lands were stunned. Pilgrims from Rome, Mesopotamia, and Egypt, as well as parts of Asia and Africa wondered how these men from Galilee could speak their languages. Many in the crowd thought the disciples might have had a little too much harvest wine (verse 13).

But Peter laid to rest any doubts when he declared,
These men are not drunk, as you suppose…. No, this is what was spoken by the prophet Joel.

"In the last days," God says,
  "I will pour out my Spirit on all people,
Your sons and daughters will prophesy,
    your young men will see visions,
    your old men will dream dreams."
      (verses 15-17)

The good news Peter went on to announce that day was embraced by almost three thousand people—both native Jews and converts to Judaism from other countries. These men and women who became followers of Jesus would usher in a new era—the Church Age—when God's saving grace would be available to all people, regardless of their ethnic or religious heritage.

To fully appreciate this moment in history and to understand God's eternal plan for His church, we must move beyond the supernatural events that took place in Jerusalem more than two thousand years ago and travel into the twenty-first century. (The maps in the appendix will help you track our journey through the Middle East.)

Our journey begins in the eastern deserts of Parthia, or modern-day Iran, formerly known as Persia. The Islamic Republic of Iran has a population of more than sixty-six million and, like ancient Parthia, has significant geopolitical influence in the world. Prior to the Islamic Revolution in 1979, there were few Muslim converts to Christianity. But in recent decades, many Shia Muslims have come to faith in Christ despite the persecution they face at the hands of Islamic extremists and Iran's oppressive regime. The Christian church is growing in this part of the world, as my colleague Phillip and I discovered when we delivered Arabic Bibles to the thriving fellowship of believers in Tehran.

From Tehran, our journey takes us through northwestern Iran, the land of the ancient Medes. Following high-altitude trade routes along the ancient Silk Road, we traverse the snow-capped Zagros Mountains that straddle the Iran-Iraq border. At a border crossing into the Kurdistan region of northern Iraq—the ancient land of Elam—heavily armed Peshmerga guards, dressed in traditional khaki harem trousers and head dresses, inspect passports before visitors are permitted entry into the land of the Kurds.

Beyond this checkpoint lies Erbil, the Kurdish capitol of Iraq. Believed to be one of the oldest inhabited cities in the world, Erbil has become the center of economic growth in Iraq. In recent years, it has also seen a spiritual revival among Orthodox and Chaldean believers, as well as an explosion of Kurdish Muslims coming to Christ. Five Kurdish congregations are currently thriving in Erbil and northern Iraq.[1]

Our journey west from Erbil takes us into more dangerous territory. The city of Mosul in northern Iraq is located on the site of ancient Nineveh, where the prophet Jonah preached. Abdul, the priest of a local mosque whose story we read about earlier, continues to secretly live out his faith in Mosul. In this land between the Tigris and Euphrates rivers—formerly Mesopotamia—sixty Iraqi pastors and Christ-followers recently gathered for a Bible conference. Many of those attending had traveled from cities in central and southern Iraq like Baghdad, Najaf, Nasiriyah, and Basra—also part of the ancient land of Elam. The need for this conference became apparent when one prominent Iraqi pastor pleaded, "Brothers, our nets are so full, we cannot pull them in fast enough. Please come and help us!"

From northwestern Iraq, our journey continues westward across the wild and rugged Taurus Mountains into modern-day Turkey—the biblical regions of Cappadocia, Pontus, Asia Minor, Phrygia, and Pamphylia. Turkey was once the land of the Hittites (Genesis 10:15), and in New Testament times, the apostle Paul established the church there (see Acts 10:26, and Revelation 2 and 3).

Located in the former region of Pontus are modern-day Istanbul, Turkey's capitol city, and the neighboring cities of Izmit and Yalova. It was in Yalova where I first met my Iraqi friend Malak, who ministered to Kurdish and Iraqi refugees following the devastating earthquake in 1999.

Following Turkey's coastline south toward Syria, we pass through the ancient city of Antioch, where followers of Jesus were first called Christians (Acts 11:26). Christianity was the dominant religion in that area for more than one thousand years until the rise of the Ottoman Empire (1350–1890), when the followers of Islam conquered the Christians in bloody religious wars. Today, Turkey is a secular Islamic country, and yet a thriving evangelical Christian community is growing there, with seventy-six churches and more than three thousand Turkish believers.

Traveling further south through the cedar forests of the Druids, the coastal cities of Syria, and the rolling hills of southern Lebanon—the territory of Hezbollah—we pass through the Israeli Defense Forces (IDF) checkpoints in the Golan Heights near the southwestern border of Syria. Crossing into Palestine and the ancient region of Galilee, Jesus' homeland, we enter the Holy Land. The former districts of Samaria, where Jesus met the woman at the well, and Judea are located to the south, bordering the Jordan River and the Dead Sea on the west. These areas belonged to the tribe of Judah in Old Testament days but were annexed by Jordan during the 1948 Arab-Israeli War, when it was renamed the West Bank. Today, more than 4.6 million Palestinians call this land home, including Wahdi and his family, whom I visited in Bethlehem.

Many Palestinians, who lost their homes during the wars with Israel in 1948 and 1967, became bitter and disenfranchised. When the people became disillusioned with Islamic extremist groups like Hamas, Hezbollah, and the PLO, the seeds for a spiritual revival began to grow in the West Bank. Today, at least twenty Palestinian Christian house churches meet in West Bank towns on a regular basis. The young believers I met at the Ramallah Teahouse in Ramallah are also reaching out to their people, offering hope through the gospel of Christ and seeking to break down the dividing wall—the Wall of Tears—that separates Palestinians from God and the rest of the world.

Skirting the Mediterranean coastline along the Gaza Strip, we travel on to the biblical land of Pharaohs and pyramids—Egypt. Long before this ancient region was conquered by Muslims in AD 640, Christianity took root through the ministry of the apostle Mark, who was martyred in Alexandria near the Nile Delta around AD 68.

In spite of almost two millennia of persecution and hardship, the Christian church in Egypt has survived to this day. In fact, the Egyptian (Coptic) church is one of the oldest surviving churches in the twenty-first century. With a population of more than one million Protestants, the roots of Christianity remain strong in Egypt.

Christian television has promoted the growth of the church, and one of the largest networks in the Middle East—SAT-7—beams in quality programs about Jesus every day. More than ten million Egyptians have access to the gospel through uncensored satellite programming.[2] Even impoverished areas like El Shahid, where Pastor Abdullah's congregation is reaching out to the Muslim community, have seen an increase in the number of believers in recent years.

Our journey ends in Egypt, but the gospel Peter preached that day in Jerusalem spread beyond this land to Arabia, Cyrene (modern-day Libya), the island of Crete, and across the Mediterranean to Rome. Millennia later, it has expanded throughout Africa to places like Khartoum, Sudan, where believers like Osama are training to share the gospel with their people, and to the farthest reaches of the globe. But no matter how far the gospel has spread around the world, its birthplace was the Middle East, among the descendants of Abraham and Ishmael.

God has not forgotten the people of the Middle East, and His plan for them is unfolding before our eyes even today!

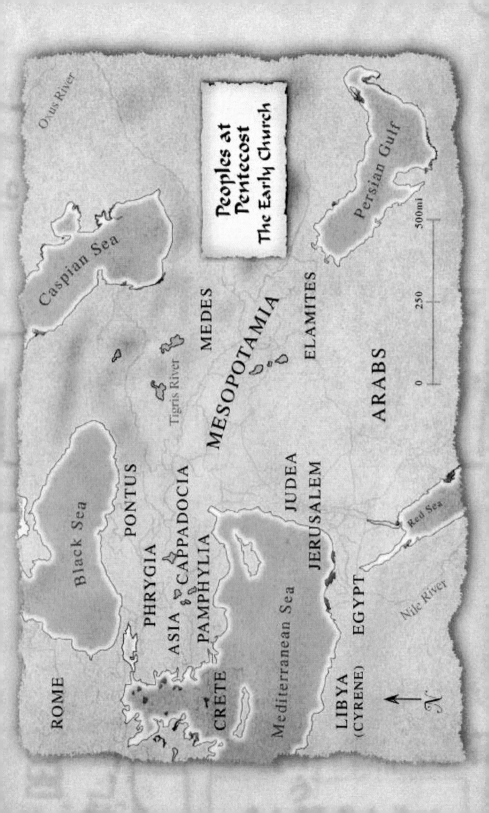

Peoples at Pentecost
The Early Church

Orus River

Caspian Sea

Persian Gulf

500mi

250

0

MEDES

MESOPOTAMIA

ELAMITES

Tigris River

ARABS

PONTUS

Black Sea

PHRYGIA

ASIA CAPPADOCIA

PAMPHYLIA

JUDEA

JERUSALEM

Red Sea

ROME

CRETE

Mediterranean Sea

EGYPT

LIBYA
(CYRENE)

Nile River

N

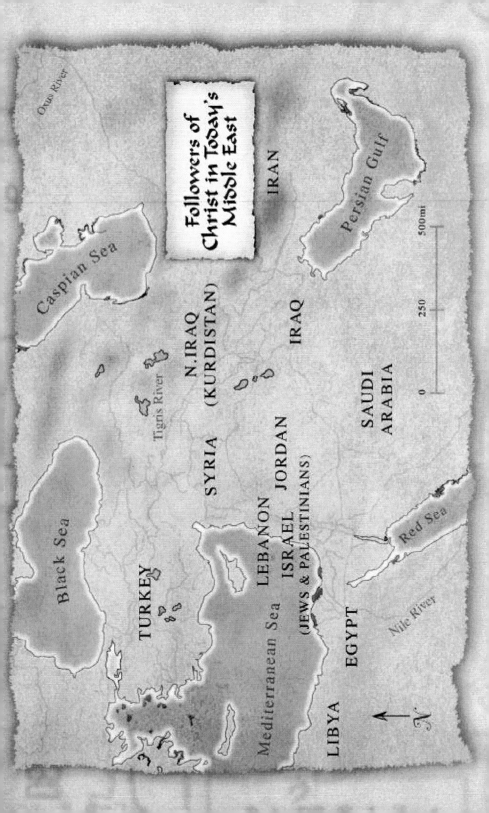

Followers of Christ in Today's Middle East

Oxus River

Caspian Sea

IRAN

Persian Gulf

Black Sea

Tigris River

N.IRAQ (KURDISTAN)

SYRIA

IRAQ

SAUDI ARABIA

TURKEY

LEBANON

JORDAN

ISRAEL (JEWS & PALESTINIANS)

Mediterranean Sea

Red Sea

EGYPT

LIBYA

Nile River

N

0   250   500mi

Prayer conference - Iraq

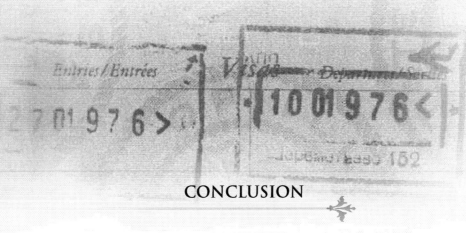

CONCLUSION

Loving the Forgotten Sons

As I've traveled around the United States sharing stories of Muslims coming to faith in Christ throughout the Middle East, people often tell me that my presentations are inspiring and challenging. But as inspiring as these stories may be, what matters most to me is what people do with the information.

I could fill several volumes with real-life accounts like the ones in this book, describing the amazing, often miraculous ways God is revealing Himself to Muslims in the twenty-first century, and yet never accomplish my ultimate goal. Don't get me wrong! I want you to feel inspired and challenged by the stories in this book. But more than anything else, I desire for these stories to transform you! I pray that God will give you a heart transplant, like the one he gave Pastor

Tom, and open your eyes to see Muslims through His eyes! I hope that you will come away from this experience not only with a new understanding of the Middle East but also with a new vision for reaching out to Muslims.

As Christians, we can no longer afford to sit on the sidelines while God is transforming hearts and lives throughout the Muslim world. We need to be engaged in sharing the love of Christ with Muslims, no matter how challenging it may seem!

In this final chapter, I want to move beyond the stories and stimulating commentary to specific steps I believe we need to take to understand God's heart for Muslims, to align ourselves with His plan, and to nurture a passion for reaching out to them with His love and grace.

ASKING GOD TO OPEN OUR EYES

First, we need to the Holy Spirit to open our eyes and give us a new perspective on the Islamic world. We need to see Muslims through His eyes, but this can only happen if God's truth comes alive in our hearts. What does God's Word say about His heart for the world?

> The LORD does not look at the things man looks at. Man looks at the outward appearance, *but the LORD looks at the heart.* (1 Samuel 16:7, emphasis added)

> For God so loved the world that he gave his one and only Son, that *whoever* believes in him shall not perish but have eternal life. (John 3:16, emphasis added)

> I urge [you to pray *for all people*].... This is good, and

pleases God our Savior, who wants [*everyone*] to be saved and to come to a knowledge of the truth. (1 Timothy 2:1, 3-4, emphasis added)

The Lord is not slow in keeping his promise, as some understand slowness. He is patient with you, *not wanting anyone to perish, but everyone to come to repentance.* (2 Peter 3:9, emphasis added)

The Bible tells us that Jesus loves *all* people and died on the cross for *everyone*. If God doesn't want *anyone* to perish, doesn't this include Muslims? If Jesus laid down His life *for everyone*, shouldn't we be willing to lay down our lives to reach Muslims? If the apostle Paul exhorts us to pray *for all people*, shouldn't we pray for the Middle East as well?

Do you realize that believers from *every* ethnic tribe and nation on the face of the earth will be worshiping God in heaven? Revelation 7:9 says that heaven will be filled with people from "every nation, tribe…and language." Surely this includes the descendants of Ishmael! God's plan for them was set in motion long before the creation of the world. The prophet Isaiah even declared that the people of Kedar and Nebaioth—a reference to the descendants of Ishmael and his two oldest sons—would one day worship the Lord in Jerusalem (Isaiah 60:7).

No doubt the Holy Spirit was looking down the halls of time to a future redemptive gathering of the Gentiles to Christ—including the Arab people. What a joyful thought that we will spend eternity with our Middle Eastern brothers and sisters in Christ! So rather than judging by external appearances and stereotyping people from this part of the world as Islamic extremists or terrorists, let's seek to understand how God sees them.

In my travels, I've often seen firsthand the profiling of people from the Middle East. On one trip just after 9/11, I was waiting to board a Lufthansa flight from Philadelphia to Frankfurt, Germany, when I noticed two young Arab men wearing long white robes and headscarves. They showed no signs of hostility as they read their Korans in the waiting area, but their presence was causing great discomfort for those around them. I watched intently as people monitored their every move with looks of anxiety and suspicion on their faces.

When the passengers started boarding the plane, the Arab men were pulled aside, hand-searched, and made to wait until everyone else had boarded. As I passed them, I couldn't help but notice the humiliation on their faces.

Seeing the world through God's eyes means refusing to judge people by the way they dress, by the color of their skin, or by the customs they practice. Our perspective is influenced by a number of factors, including our culture, our values and prejudices, our faith background, and our experiences. We see the world through our own preset filters, but God looks beyond mere appearances to the heart!

How can you learn to see the world through God's eyes?

1. Discover how God sees the world by searching His Word and seeking to understand Him better as you pray for Him to open your eyes. God created all cultures with their unique characteristics, and He sees each person through eyes of love

and grace.

2. Challenge your own perceptions of the world by comparing them with God's view. (Of course, you have to know what your perceptions are before you can challenge them!)

3. Consider looking at the world from a different vantage point by learning about other cultures and faiths.

Asking God to Give Us an Open Mind

Second, we need an open mind so that we can engage Muslims in an informed way as we seek to share God's love with them. As Westerners, we often fear or become suspicious of what we don't understand. This is especially true of how we view Muslims and Islam in general.

Our views of Muslims are often formed by what we read and see in the media, but how much do we truly know about them? As I mentioned earlier in the book, many Americans think that all Muslims are terrorists or extremists, but if we take a closer look, we realize that they are people just like us, who need to experience God's life-transforming grace.

When we take the time to learn about their culture and faith, we'll be able to relate to Muslims with respect and compassion rather than suspicion and fear. God has given believers "a spirit of power, of love and of self-discipline" (2 Timothy 1:7), not a spirit of fear. His Word reminds us that "there is no fear in love. But perfect love [God's love] drives out fear" (1 John 4:18). (We'll talk more about loving Muslims in the next section.)

To better understand people from the Middle East so that we can relate to them without fear and suspicion, we first need to ask God to open our minds and transform the way we think about the Muslim world. As we seek the mind of Christ, God will enable us to understand and relate to Muslims with His love and discernment (1 Corinthians 2:16). We also need a teachable spirit and an inquisitive mind. Researching the following questions is one way to broaden our understanding of Muslims:

- ~ What are the customs and beliefs of Muslims in the Middle East and in other parts of the world?

- ~ In what ways are we alike and different?

- ~ What are the differences and similarities between Islam and Christianity?

- ~ What are the felt needs and spiritual longings of Muslims?

Reading about Islam and Muslim culture is one of the best ways to nurture a broader understanding of Muslims in the Middle East and here in America. To get you started, I've provided a list of recommended reading in the back of the book.

ASKING GOD FOR AN OPEN HEART

Just as God is able to open our eyes and minds to see the Muslim people from His perspective, He can also transform our hearts, filling them with His love and compassion for everyone. Loving people we may think of as our enemies is impossible in our own strength, but the Holy Spirit can empower us to love those who hate us. We show that we truly belong to the Lord when we reflect His heart for the world around us.

Jesus said, "Love your enemies, do good to those who hate you, bless those who curse you, pray for those who mistreat you.... Be merciful just as your Father is merciful" (Luke 6:27–28, 36). Not surprisingly, a growing number of Muslims are responding to the gospel because Christians have shown genuine love and concern for them. The concept of a loving God is foreign to most Muslims. According to the Koran, Allah is a God of judgment and unapproachable holiness, so a demonstration of God's love often has a powerful impact on Muslims.

I discovered the impact of genuine love firsthand on one of my first trips to Chechnya. During my visit, a Chechen security agent was assigned to accompany me as my bodyguard. For such a burly man, Mustafa was amazingly gentle and quiet mannered. He seemed genuinely interested in making sure I remained safe.

On one occasion, after an intense day of navigating through military checkpoints and evading other dangers, Mustafa and I enjoyed a moment of relaxation over cups of hot black tea. After finishing his tea, Mustafa removed his leather jacket and gun holster and unloaded his Makarov pistol. Laying it carefully on the table, he rolled out a small prayer rug on the floor in an adjoining room and, as a faithful Muslim, recited his evening prayers.

When he returned to the table, he looked me straight in the eyes and asked, "David, why did you come to Chechnya? You are a Christian. Russians are also Christian, and they kill us. Christians and Muslims hate one another."

"Mustafa," I replied, "I came to tell you and your people that

God loves you. He isn't American or Chechen or Russian. He loves all people the same way, and He wants everyone to know Him and the peace He offers through His Son, Jesus."

Mustafa considered my words and then asked about my family. When I told him that they wanted to join me on a future visit, he seemed surprised at first and then declared emphatically, "You must not bring your wife and children here! They are safe in America. You cannot place them in danger! Our wives and children are not safe here!"

"Does God love my wife and children more than yours?" I asked. "My family wants to come to Chechnya to share His love for your family and the Chechen people."

Mustafa stared at the floor in silence. Finally he lifted his eyes and said, "David, I have been a Muslim all my life, and I have never seen this kind of love among Muslims. Your God is love; my God is angry."

That day I realized that love in action is one of the most powerful ways to share Jesus with Muslims.

God's love and human love are worlds apart. The difference between God's love and human love is this: We love because we get something in return; God loves us because He is love (1 John 4:16). In His sacrificial love, God gave His only Son for those who turned away from Him. Scripture tells us that "God demonstrated his own love for us in this: While we were still sinners, Christ died for us" (Romans 5:8). The love of Christ is the only love that can reach the Muslim world.

How can you nurture an open heart toward Muslims?

- By remembering who you were before Jesus saved you. Each of us was separated from the love of God at one time, and if God loved us in all our sinfulness and spiritual poverty, He loves the Muslim people too.

- By seeking to become more like Jesus. The only way you can do this is to draw closer to Him, surrender to the Holy Spirit's work in your life, and immerse yourself in His Word.

- By asking God to correct any heart attitudes toward Muslims that don't reflect His love, including prejudice and spiritual pride.

One of the biggest obstacles that can hinder us from reaching out to Muslims is an attitude of spiritual pride and superiority. Jesus exposed this attitude in the disciples' hearts when He reached out to a Samaritan woman, who belonged to an ethnic group the Jews considered defiled and spiritually inferior (John 4:1-42). Jesus added insult to injury when he asked this woman for a drink of water and had a life-giving conversation with her.

The disciples were far more concerned about this woman defiling their white-washed image than they were about her value to God. They completely missed the lesson Jesus wanted them to learn: God offers salvation to both Jews and Gentiles, and He longs for all people to worship Him in spirit and in truth. In God's kingdom, there is no room for spiritual pride. Salvation is a gift we receive by faith, not because of our own righteousness or because we're better than another ethnic or religious group. (See Ephesians 2:8-9 and Titus 3:4-5.)

That day at the well of Sychar, Jesus offered living water to the

Samaritan people and challenged His disciples to peel the religious scales from their eyes to see the fields that were ready to be harvested. Through this unlikely encounter, Jesus revealed His heart for the world. No one is spiritually inferior or unreachable in His eyes. The love of Christ extends to all, because all of us are sinners in need of a Savior!

How can you guard against religious pride?

1. Ask God to remove any traces of religious pride and superiority from your heart.

2. Recognize in a spirit of humility that God's family is made up of all races and ethnicities. In Christ, "there is neither Jew nor Greek [nor descendant of Ishmael], slave nor free, male nor female, for [we] are all one in [Him]" (Galatians 3:28).

Confronting Misguided Patriotism

Webster's dictionary defines *patriotism* as "love of country or kingdom with a corresponding willingness to sacrifice for the good of all, even to the point of laying down one's life." But all too often, modern-day patriotism seems to equate love of country with hatred not only of its enemies—real or perceived—but of any culture or people group that doesn't share our values, customs, or faith. Patriotism in and of itself isn't wrong, but it's wrong when it becomes a justification to hate others.

Howard Thurman, a respected author and civil-rights leader, once said, "During times of war, hatred becomes quite respectable, even though it has to masquerade...under the guise of patriotism."

But for followers of Christ, hatred should never be respectable, even if it's considered patriotic! True patriotism is characterized by love and forgiveness. Martin Luther King Jr. once said,

> He who is devoid of the power to forgive is devoid of the power to love. There is some good in the worst of us and some evil in the best of us. When we discover this, we are less prone to hate our enemies.

A powerful example of forgiveness in modern times is the story of Edith Cavell, a British nurse who helped two hundred Allied soldiers in Belgium escape the Germans during World War I. Facing death by a German firing squad, she uttered these amazing words of forgiveness for her executioners: "Standing, as I do, in view of God and eternity, I realize that patriotism is not enough. I must have no hatred or bitterness towards anyone."

Patriotism is not enough! Especially misguided patriotism that justifies hating our enemies.

Recently a large AM radio station invited me to speak on the air about Muslims coming to Christ in the Middle East. The timing of the interview couldn't have been more appropriate—just two days before the eighth anniversary of the 9/11 terrorist attacks.

As we talked, I sensed that one of the hosts was uneasy. Finally, with great emotion, he said, "David, your stories about Muslims coming to Christ are incredible. But how can Americans forgive those who killed so many innocent people on 9/11? We're a Christian nation that was attacked by Islamic terrorists! Truthfully, even as a Christian, I have a hard time forgiving them, and I suspect that many of our listeners do as well."

I understood his struggle.

"The answer isn't easy," I replied. "I struggle with these issues too. But as Christians we must ask ourselves a deeper question: What is patriotism, and what kingdom are we serving? Having worked among Muslims in Chechnya and other Islamic countries, I believe that only the Holy Spirit can enable me to keep my eyes fixed on the right kingdom and love those who hate me."

As followers of Christ, we belong to a different kingdom, and only one flag waves over that kingdom: the banner of love. Jesus said, "My kingdom is not of this world" (John 18:36), and neither is ours! He calls us to "seek first his kingdom and righteousness" (Matthew 6:33), even if that goes against the patriotic grain at times. God's kingdom transcends nationality, and loving Him and our neighbors must take first place in our hearts, even before love of country (Matthew 22:37–39).

Don't get me wrong! Loving and serving God doesn't mean that we shouldn't love our country or defend her with our very lives if called upon to do so. It simply means that our first allegiance as believers is to Christ and His kingdom. In a time of war, our kingdom priorities can easily get off track, and our perspective on patriotism can get skewed. We can forget that Jesus isn't wrapped in the American flag. God doesn't show favoritism toward any nationality but blesses all "who earnestly seek him." (See Acts 10:30-36; Romans 2:11; and Hebrews 11:6.)

Since 9/11, I've seen some pretty disturbing expressions of patriotism here in the States—like cartoon figures urinating on Osama bin Laden, proudly displayed on pickup trucks. But what grieves my heart most are believers who ridicule Muslims or spew hate-filled language, all in the name of patriotism. Expressions like these are not only demeaning of Middle Eastern people but are shameful behaviors for followers of Christ, who preach a gospel of love and forgiveness.

Misguided patriotism is often a sign of bitterness and unforgiveness. In the shadow of 9/11, how can we forgive those who have committed such atrocities against us? I could quote plenty of Bible verses on forgiveness and talk about other historic twentieth-century atrocities that seem impossible to forgive, but I think the best way to answer this question is to describe an encounter I had with a man from Kazakhstan in Central Asia.

After a church presentation in Spokane, Washington, Bihar approached me with tears in his eyes. "I began to learn about loving my enemies several years ago," he began. "After the fall of the Soviet Union, missionaries came to Kazakhstan and shared the gospel of Jesus Christ. My entire family became believers, and soon after this, we started a small house church to learn more about Jesus. One evening during Bible study, a group of black-hooded Muslims stormed into our house and killed four members of my family. For months I allowed hatred and bitterness for these killers to poison my heart. Then Jesus showed me that just as He forgave those who killed Him, I should forgive those who killed my family. It has been very difficult for me, but I have begun to pray for my enemies and have asked God to give me His love for them."

I was deeply moved by this man's words and the incredible display of God's forgiveness in his heart.

How can you recognize and eradicate misguided patriotism in your life? Here are a few suggestions:

1. Ask God to teach you what true patriotism is, and align your beliefs and attitudes with His truth.

2. Dig into God's Word to understand what His kingdom priorities are and see if your own priorities and allegiances are in harmony with God's. If they aren't, work on getting your focus and priorities straight.

3. Ask yourself some hard questions about how you treat Muslims. Do you demean or ridicule them, or laugh along with those who do? Do your attitudes, words, and behaviors reflect God's heart for the Muslim world or disgrace God's name and grieve the Holy Spirit?

I realize that my words in this section may offend some readers, but I felt strongly that they needed to be said. As followers of Christ, we need to guard against misguided patriotism so that He can shine His light through us to a hurting world.

Reaching Out with Open Hands

Jesus is calling us to see Muslims through his eyes, to understand who they are, and to love them in His power. But He also wants us to reach out and engage them.

Reaching out to Muslims isn't easy. Not all Muslims hate Christians, but some do. As believers, we know we're supposed to love our enemies (Luke 6:27, 35), but what does this really mean? Does God expect us to excuse what Muslim terrorists did on 9/11?

Romans 12 tells us,

Do not repay anyone evil for evil.... If it is possible, as far as it depends on you, live at peace with everyone. Do not take revenge, my friends, but leave room for God's wrath, for it is written, "It is mine to avenge; I will repay," says the Lord. On the contrary: 'If your enemy is hungry, feed him; if he is thirsty, give him something to drink.'... Do not be overcome by evil, but overcome evil with good. (verses 17, 18-20, 21)

How do God's people overcome evil with good? Through simple acts of mercy and compassion! Feeding poor families in El Shahid, Egypt; serving tea in Ramallah; teaching a Bible study in Iraq; rebuilding schools in an earthquake zone in Turkey; helping out a Muslim neighbor in the United States—all of these are examples of how we can be the hands and feet of Jesus to Muslims.

Like no other time in history, the followers of Jesus have limitless opportunities in the twenty-first century to engage the Muslim world. Westerners have access to places that would have been impossible to visit a decade ago—war zones like Iraq and Afghanistan, and areas of devastation and poverty like Chechnya, the West Bank, and Sudan.

Now that you've read the inspiring stories of Muslims who found the God they were longing to know, let's translate this inspiration into action! Here are four practical steps you can take to reach out to Muslims:

1. *Inform yourself.* There are a number of dedicated ministries working in the Muslim world today. Many of them have Web sites that describe their focus and the ways you might become involved. As you research these ministries, ask the Lord to guide you to the ones He wants you to partner with. There are also excellent books

and other media resources available for those who want to learn more about Muslims and their beliefs, as well as how to share the gospel with them. Some of these resources are listed in the appendix.

2. Intercede for missions workers, Muslims, and Muslim converts to Christianity. Even if you can't become a foreign missionary or go on a short-term missions trip to the Middle East, you can pray! Thank God for the creative ways He is reaching Muslims and ask Him to send more believers to the Islamic world to share the gospel and train indigenous pastors (Matthew 9:37). Intercede for their safety and pray for good relationships with the Muslim people they're trying to reach.

Pray that the Lord will open the hearts and eyes of Muslims to receive the gospel and that God will continue revealing Himself to them through dreams and visions. Pray, too, for former Muslims who are experiencing persecution—and even death—because of their faith in Christ. Ask God to protect them, strengthen them, and fill them with boldness and love as they tell their people about Jesus.

A prayer guide can help you pray for the specific needs of Muslims and intercede for believers in the Middle East. One well-known and very reliable guide is *Operation World.* (You can usually purchase a discounted copy online at Amazon.com or another book-distribution site.) Youth with a Mission also has an effective thirty-day prayer guide for those who want to intercede for Muslims during the holy month of Ramadan.

3. Invest financially in ministries to Muslims. In addition to praying, you can financially support the ministries that work among Muslims. The costs of living and operating a ministry in a foreign country can be staggering. Ministries not only need workers to serve around the world—and at home—but they also need financial support from those God has called to partner in this way. Even a small contribution on a regular basis can keep a ministry going that otherwise might have to close its doors for financial reasons.

4. *Get involved.* There are countless ways you can get involved in ministry to Muslims, not just overseas but in your own community. Pray about joining a short-term mission team to the Middle East. There's no better way to experience the culture and learn what God is doing among the Muslim people than to go there and see for yourself.

If Muslims live in your community, reach out to a family in your neighborhood. Invite them into your home and get to know them. Or eat at a Middle Eastern restaurant in your city, where you'll have many opportunities to meet Muslims and build friendships with them. Start a Bible study for Muslims who are interested in learning more about Jesus, or chat online with people from the Middle East. Build a relationship with a student from the Middle East who is attending a local university. Pray about how the Lord would have you get involved and then do it!

God hasn't forgotten the descendants of Ishmael, and He invites us to join Him in the great harvest that is taking place in the Muslim world today! The Lord of the harvest is calling… Will you answer?

Notes

INTRODUCTION

1. Story based on Genesis 15–18 and 21. Cultural information taken from a variety of references, including Bible dictionaries and encyclopedias. Parts of the story have been embellished to draw out aspects not reflected in the historical account.

2. See Genesis 16:3.

3. According to Genesis 12:16, Abram acquired a number of servants while in Egypt, and some scholars believe that Pharaoh may have presented Hagar to Abram as a gift. See James Orr, ed., *The International Standard Bible Encyclopedia*, vol. 2 (Grand Rapids: Eerdmans, 1956), s.v. "Hagar."

4. Historical and cultural information in the commentary was gleaned from a variety of sources, including online and print encyclopedias and Bible references.

CHAPTER 1

1. Information on the hajj taken from "Hajj: Pilgrimage to Mecca," BBC, September 8, 2009, www.bbc.co.uk/religion/religions/islam/practices/hajj_1.shtml; and "The Ka'ba, Mecca," Sacred Destinations, October 22, 2009, http://www.sacred-destinations.com/saudi-arabia/mecca-kaba.

2. The words *God* and *Allah* have been used interchangeably in some instances, since *Allah* is the Arabic word for God. The

Islamic concept of God, however, differs in many important respects from the God of the Bible. One major difference is the concept of Allah as distant and unknowable, a God not of love and relationship but of legalistic demands and unpredictability.

CHAPTER 3

1. Ken Walker, "Muslims Finding Christ Through Dreams," Charisma News Online, December 23, 2008, www.charismamag.com/index.php/news/19405%20.

CHAPTER 4

1. Statistics taken from an article on Najaf at GlobalSecurity.org, www.globalsecurity.org/military/world/iraq/najaf.htm (accessed February 4, 2010).

CHAPTER 7

1. Statistics from "Internet Usage Statistics: The Internet Big Picture," Internet World Stats, September 30, 2009, www.internetworldstats.com.

CHAPTER 11

1. Historical information on Ramallah in this section was taken from a variety of online sources, including Wikipedia (http://en.wikipedia.org/wiki/Ramallah) and http://ramallahpalestine.net/History_of_Ramallah.html.

CHAPTER 12

1. Historical information in this section was taken from a variety of online sources, including Wikipedia.

2. "Warrant Issued for Sudan's Leader," BBC News, March 4, 2009, http://news.bbc.co.uk/2/hi/africa/7923102.stm.

3. Patrick Johnstone and Jason Mandryk, *Operation World: When We Pray God Works* (Cumbria, UK: Paternoster Lifestyle, 2001), 596.

CHAPTER 13

1. See Acts 16:16-25.

2. Information about the gods of Egypt taken from *Nelson's Complete Book of Bible Maps and Charts* (Nashville: Thomas Nelson, 1996), 25–27.

CHAPTER 15

1. Information on the number of churches and believers in the Middle East in this chapter has been taken from Patrick Johnstone and Jason Mandryk, *Operation World: When We Pray God Works* (Cumbria, UK: Paternoster Lifestyle, 2001).

2. Johnstone and Mandryk, *Operation World.*